Unraveling the
Spreading Cloth of Time:

Indigenous Thoughts
Concerning The Universe

MariJo Moore

Trace A. Demeyer

rENEGADE pLANETS pUBLISHING

Candler, NC, USA

Also by Trace A. DeMeyer

One Small Sacrifice: A Memoir; Blue Hand Books, MA

Two Worlds: Lost Children of the Indian Adoption Projects; co-edited by Patricia Busbee; Blue Hand Books, MA

Sleeps With Knives, poetry chapbook/penname Laramie Harlow; Blue Hand Books, MA

Also by MariJo Moore

A Book of Spiritual Wisdom – for all days

A Book of Ceremonies and Spiritual Energies Thereof

The Boy With A Tree Growing From His Ear and Other Stories

The Diamond Doorknob

When The Dead Dream

Confessions of a Madwoman

Confessions of a Madwoman – an oral journey

Red Woman With Backward Eyes and Other Stories

Spirit Voices of Bones

Returning to the Homeland: Cherokee Poetry and Short Stories

Desert Quotes

Crow Quotes

Tree Quote

Bear Quotes

All by rENEGADE pLANETS pUBLISHING

By additional publishers:

The Ice Man; Rigby Publishers/Houghton Mifflin, MA

The First Fire; Rigby Publishers/Houghton Mifflin, MA

The Cherokee Little People; Rigby Publishers/Houghton Mifflin, MA

Genocide of the Mind: New Native Writings; Nation Books, NYC (Ed.)

Eating Fire, Tasting Blood: Breaking the Great Silence of the American Indian Holocaust; Thunder's Mouth Press, NYC (Ed.)

Birthed From Scorched Hearts; Women Respond to War; Fulcrum Publishing, CO (Ed.)

Feeding the Ancient Fires: A Collection of Writings by North Carolina American Indians; NC Humanities Council, NC (Ed.)

Unraveling the Spreading Cloth of Time:
Indigenous Thoughts Concerning the Universe

Published by
rENEGADE pLANETS pUBLISHING
PO Box 2493
Candler, NC 28715
www.marijomoore.com

March 2013
Compilation Copyright MariJo Moore
Cover art "We Know Much More Than We Allow Ourselves to Believe" mixed media collage, Copyright MariJo Moore, 2013

ISBN:9781483952871
Library of Congress Control Number: 2013904416

Layout and design by Phil Olson, Asheville, NC

Printed in the USA

Contents

Part One
Our Universe Consists of the Interconnectedness of
All Elements, Organisms, Thoughts, the Seen and Unseen,
Known and Unknown in Perpetual Cyclical Time

Part Two
Cosmologies of Indigenous Medicine, Ceremonialism and Perspectives Therefore

Part Three
Prayers, Dreams, Visions, Songs, Dances, Birth and Death: Beckoning the Nucleus of The Great Mystery

Part Four

Stories Old and New, Told and Retold, Spinning and Spinning, Keeping the Universe Intact

Part Five
Pathways of Sacred Spaces and Spiritual Energies

Introduction

"All the tribes say the universe is just the product of mind … It fits perfectly with the quantum. Indians believe the universe is mind, but they explore the spiritual end of it, not the physical end."

Vine Deloria Jr.

This anthology does not reveal secret "how-to's" concerning the ceremonies of Indigenous peoples, neither does it reveal the "power" of medicine people, nor reveal knowledge meant to be kept in tribal protection. There is certain sacred knowledge from all Indigenous cultures that should never be written, which should only be passed on orally to those who are capable of the responsibility. Regardless, this anthology gives credence that Indigenous peoples have put into practice (for millenniums) what most physicists and scientists have considered only as theories. Exploring Quantum physics in relation to Indigenous peoples' understanding of the spiritual universe, these writings include personal experiences, traditional stories, fictional and nonfiction ponderings, beliefs, and explorations. In no way do these cover all aspects of Indigenous thoughts, nor do they represent all Indian nations, or speak for all Indigenous peoples.

The universe is complex; of this there is no doubt. However, most Indigenous people know there are natural laws that remain true, regardless of who or what applies them. We know these laws because we, as our ancestors, respect them, honor them, and return to them. This is not to say we hold all the answers to the mysteries of the world; that is not possible at this stage of the human race. But we do believe in the mysteries of the universe, even if they cannot be "proved" mathematically or scientifically. We believe because we were taught to believe. Our definition of "science" is definitely relative to cultural beliefs. As noted Anishinaabe elder storyteller Basil H. Johnston relates, "From the phenomenon they saw and heard, touched and tasted, smelled and sensed, our grandfathers and grandmothers made up stories for the understanding. Thousands of stories did they store in their memories leaving us, their descendants, with a good grasp of the natural world."

Indigenous people understand that a spiritual force that cannot be destroyed connects one and all. In other words, we do not have and have never had theories: we practice what we believe not only because we were taught to believe, but because of accepted innate wisdom. There is balance: there is light – there is darkness. There is life – there is death. There is rebirth – there is re-death. All that goes around comes around.

Time is not linear; time is cyclical. There is stillness – there is movement. There is confusion. There is clarity. There is space. There is time.

Lakota author Amy Krout-Horn explains, "I feel that time is the acknowledgement, the awareness of transition, transformation, and change, existing as continuous motion, unending movement, flowing around us, through us, connecting everything in a spiraling dance within another dance within another dance."

Thousands of distinct Indigenous languages have been silenced forever due to pandemics of smallpox and other diseases brought by European contact, acculturation, and total annihilation. Although there are agendas in action by many nations to revive their languages, some linguists have estimated that perhaps there are forty to fifty years left before all Native languages are completely gone if they continue to dissipate at the rate they have over the past hundred years. Traditional languages are the crux of cultural perspective, a way of "viewing the world." A system of acknowledging that everything is in constant flux, and everything that exists does so in interrelationships. Please note, in some traditional languages, there is no word for time as defined by Western science. Of course, Indigenous thoughts written in English cannot directly reveal Indigenous paradigm; nonetheless, this book is an offer to assist in a deeper explanation.

From various tribal creation stories to the Maya and Hopi declarations of the emergence of new worlds, Indigenous peoples have explanations of how this universe exists and evolves. And so, this collection will end where it begins: sharing our Indigenous thoughts, questions, answers and dreams with others. We will come full circle...circular, just as time continues on its cyclical path.

Dedicated to Lakota literary genius, visionary, and groundbreaking Indigenous activist, Vine Deloria Jr., this anthology assures his aspiration for the continuance of sharing Indigenous perceptions.

Sing Your Song for Vine
(For the Celebration of the Life of Vine Deloria Jr., 11/18/05)

suzan shown harjo

Vine was our sacred mountain and raging river and gentle rain
    Healing sage after Sun Dance sacrifice
    Cool, calm waters after a hard day's work

He was that wicked funny thought at the least appropriate time
    Whip smart and Coyote clever
    Tossing banana peels beneath the feet of the pompous

He was our Atticus Finch
    Who defended us to the death
He was our teasing cousin
    Who never let us get away with pretension
Our kind grandpa
    Who wanted us to love each other
Our warrior leader
    Who lifted us up for counting coup
Our stern teacher
    Who made us sit up straight

Our good-time uncle
　Who took us to old-timey movies
Our kid brother
　Who always wanted to play another game

He filled our horizons and now we see him as a mirage
　But, sing your song for Vine and call him to your side
　A Yanktonai song for the longest journey
　An honor song of praise and thanksgiving
　A traveling song by the Sons of the Pioneers
Then, he will be there
　As a shadow of an eagle overhead
　As the glint of silver medicine flying from the
　corner of your eye
　As a distant sound that commands your attention
　As a sudden realization you might think is an original idea
　As the turning aspen leaves in the peace and glory of the
　dying moment
　As a gentle voice telling you things will be better when
　you know they never will be
　As, maybe, just a sigh
　　Ah, hello, my dear friend
　　I have a song for you

Aho.

Part One

Our Universe Consists of the
Interconnectedness of All Elements,
Organisms, Thoughts, the Seen and
Unseen, Known and Unknown in
Perpetual Cyclical Time

Our lives are described and explained by our experiences.
The belief is: we are part of everything; therefore we exist in the
centeredness of this principle. One action affects another and
this connects with another and this other reaches another and
so on…much like integrated strands of a spider's web.

Although there is great diversity among the actions, cultures
and traditions of Indigenous peoples, there is no such thing as
isolation. Even if we cannot "know" everything concerning the
universe, we are still an integral part of it. We gain experiential
knowledge, which becomes inner wisdom.

Everything that exists is fused by time. Time is a spiritual
pulsating rhythm evolving in cosmic spaces. All is an aspect of
the universe's dreamtime.

My Son, You Are a Part of This Forever

gabriel horn

It had begun its voyage so long ago from a place too far away for us to imagine. They say that it had traveled from the Mystery to this time of Everything That Is Now.

It had journeyed past distant quasars and pulsars, super novas, and spiral galaxies of countless suns, and myriad worlds and moons. It moved on and on, appearing like a white shell bead in the darkness of heaven, skimming just out of reach of mammoth black holes and worm holes, on and on, sailing silent and solitary across a celestial sea of endless space.

A frozen speck of cosmic dust, it would one day cross the path of our father, the Sun. Thus warmed in his heat, it would dissolve from ice, melting into the cloud stuff of heavy mist. In the heat of the father's light, they say, "...the great mist-clouds thickened together and fell," and that a droplet of divine wisdom descended into the newborn sea, amalgamating within the womb of our Mother, gestating and awaiting substance and form.

It is said that in the perpetual motion of her ever-changing cycles and movements, she had gathered from the depths of her waters the *power of creation. "…Then did the Sun-father take council within himself, and casting his glance downward espied, on the great waters, a Foam-cap near to the Earth-mother. With his beam he impregnated and with his heat incubated the Foam-cap, whereupon she gave birth…."*

And thus, they say, all beings, great and small, born of this union would inherently understand that they shared life with all things and were related to all life. This was the pristine wisdom carried in the comet's seed.

****

"All things born of the Earth belong to the Earth," I said, kneeling near the shore on a finger of land that extended into the water. A wrapped bundle lay just above the shallow hole I had dug earlier in the sand. In the methodic rush of the rising tide, a persistent breeze twirled the heron feathers tied around my arms, lifting my long hair, and mingling with the scent of the maternal blood.

In the slowly lightening horizon, golden strokes of the unseen Sun brushed the underside of the billowy ashen clouds, and caused me to smile.

Then I turned and searched into the firmament, exploring the eternal blackness that reached beyond the sphere of my existence, extending farther than my human ability to either comprehend or imagine; where boundaries in any form no longer existed.

It was in that space of greatest abstraction where the night hung back and where the immense vastness encountered forever that the most far-a-away stars had still availed themselves, affirming the inner truth I had come to know: that the purpose of my life was reaching fruition, and that what belonged to the Earth also belonged to the Mystery. It did not belong to me.

As water seeped in from the bottom of the hole, I pushed the sand back, filling it, and burying the placenta.

With the crescent Moon hanging low, I lifted the small bundle, and pulling myself up, stepped closer to the water's edge where a sliver of light extended into a thin shimmering trail that led from where I was standing to the mysteries that lay beyond. "You are part of this, *Ihasha*," I said, raising the bundle with the tiny being wrapped inside. Then I drew the bundle close, and cradling it, my gaze shifted from the horizon to the infant's face to where a single white shell bead was secured to a string of turquoise around his neck. As a strong gust blew his wispy hair just above his blinking eyes of black liquid jade, I smiled again. "You are part of everything that is known," I said, "and everything as a man you can never know."

With the bundle still pressed to my chest, I focused once

more on the grand expanse of the Sea before us. "You belong to all of this," I said while past, present, and future all at once merged in my awareness to become One moment within this One complete thought. "All of this is forever a part of you, and you are forever a part of this."

As I stood in the fading trail of Moonlight, I brimmed with a love and remembrance that radiated from every part that was me at that instant and every part that would evermore live within me.

Then I set the baby down, and, spreading my arms like a heron opening its wings, I motioned over the dunes that reconnected me to the land behind us and towards the sea before us. "This is our Mother," I affirmed. "She is the water born of the Mystery. She is the Ocean, and she is the land that emerges from the water. She is the water that is you. She is the whole world. Everything belongs to her that is born of her."

With my focus shifting to the fading glimmer of those lasting stars that still clung to their place even before the rising and mighty sun, when points of light surpass the boundaries of time, I paused. "But, there is more," I said.

Images of thoughts and feelings of my own life's journey appeared and disappeared: the times of heartache and loss that I had endured; the occasions when I had remained determined despite the circumstances of obstruction; the struggle to understand my own place in it all, and the hope that was now wrapped in the sacred bundle on the sand.

"And you belong to them, my son," I said, lifting the infant, gesturing to the stars. "Nothing can be more certain than this. See it! See it, *Ihasha*! See the Mystery for the wonder that it is, and know it is the wonder in you."

In silence, I, a man who was becoming a father, rested. As the waves broke in soothing sound and the wind settled in quiet transition and the faint trail of Moonlight dissipated into a golden dawn, I readied myself within the quiet calm. Then, walking towards where there was no visible path, I climbed over the dunes, cradling a new life with all the hope that its primal wisdom never be forgotten.

****

A seemingly endless flow of seasons and tides have faded into the Mystery of Time, and as I reflect on the way the moonlight still shines a shimmering trail out to that place where the horizon meets the Mystery, I am once again aware of my own place within it all. In a few days, *Ihasha* will graduate with honors from the University of South Florida. He will take with him the learning of the Western world, but I know that the technological nature of that knowledge will not serve him as he explores the nature of his own existence. Therein dwells another kind of knowing, another kind of honor.

Kneeling in the water, I pat my open hands gently upon her surface. It is a ritual of tender solicitude. The dolphins had taught this to me when anger once filled my heart. In that prayerful moment, as the dolphins swam around me, I cried my gratitude to them and to all life that still remained despite the actions of civilized men. Now, as my eyes scan the horizon, instinctively expecting to see an emerging dorsal in the moonlight, I am still grateful, though I understand that too many people who share this life with *Ihasha* will never be compelled to place their hands in appreciation upon the water this way. Having intellectually severed their ties to the Earth, generations become hardened, as their machines make them soft. They become further isolated, as they crowd into more confining places. They become victims to their illusions of superiority that in their minds and hearts detach them from everything.

My faith in the ceremony that first brought me to these shores with my son shall not be the desperate act of a man whose indigenous way of seeing the world and the universe is dying, but an affirmation of determination in that indigenous way of seeing.

And as the sound of Time merges in the rush of water forever flowing it seems in and out from these shores, the burst of a dolphin's breath nearby sends spray rising like mist over the sea of primal memory. *Ihasha will remember.* This I say because I know this like the ocean knows the rain.

At the corner of my eye, a particle of starlight trails across the sapphire Sky at the same time a wave wraps around me. Both particle and wave exists at the precise moment of acknowledgment and gratitude, in this sacred moment of Everything That Is Now.

Excerpted and adapted from the award-winning novella, *Transcendence,* All Things That Matter Press © Gabriel Horn, 2009. Printed here with permission of the author.

Listening

John Trudell

"We are forms of the earth… all things and forms of the earth are made of the same metals minerals and liquids …Earth is our mother …All our Relations. The being part of human and all other forms is our relationship to sun sky universe… Life is a form of the energy of being…"

I was listening
To the voices of life
Chanting in unison
Carry on the struggle
The generations
Surge together
In resistance
To Meet
The reality of power

Mother Earth
Embraces her children
In natural beauty
To last beyond

Oppressors' brutality
As the butterfly floats into life
We are the spirit of natural life
Which is forever

The power of understanding
Real connection to spirit
Is meaning our resistance
Our struggle
Is not sacrifice lost
It is
Natural energy properly used

"Listening" was published in *Lines from a Mined Mind*, Fulcrum Publishing,
© John Trudell, 2008. Printed here with permission of the author.

Deciphering the Great Mystery

Dean Hutchins

Eurasian scientists and philosophers have long sought to understand the meaning of life, to understand why we are here and how the Universe works. For centuries, various disciplines have battled one another, each promoting their own theories as the truth. It was not until the 20th Century that they began to suspect something that the Indigenous peoples of the Western Hemisphere have known all along. Everything is connected.

There have been great differences in approach between the people separated by the Atlantic Ocean. There may be some confusion here in using the term "Western." Europeans consider themselves a "Western" people, a term they adopted back in the 4th Century when they, living on the western peninsula of the Asian continent, believed they were the westernmost people on the planet. The term has come to apply to any country where European immigrants are the dominant culture, and the local culture is absorbed into being "Western" without credit or acknowledgement. Since Asia is considered Eastern, and Turtle Island, what is now called the Americas, is clearly geographically Western, perhaps I should be referring to Europe as Middle Earth (with apologies to J.R.R. Tolkien.) But for the purposes of this essay, I will continue with the convention of referring to Europeans as Western and the true Western peoples as Indigenous.

On the Eastern shores of the Atlantic, the peoples of the European peninsula of Asia viewed science and philosophy as separate fields of discipline and, for the greater part of their development, they not only disagreed with each other but they also had religion to contend with. Within each area of thought, gains in knowledge were used to acquire wealth and power, rather than being used for the betterment of all of society.

Philosophers searched for answers to the ultimate questions about the meaning of life. "Why are we here?" "What is reality", etc… But Western philosophers tended to view themselves outside the world, not part of the world. They wanted the world to make some sense to them on their terms, and described it in ways as if they were critics sitting in a theater, viewing the world as a piece of performance art.

These critics started out well. Aristotle, for example, believed that thinking makes you immortal, and Socrates declared that the only true wisdom consists in knowing that you know nothing. Socrates' search for truth however, brought him into conflict with the religious thinking of the day and he was sentenced to death.

Plato however, following in Socrates' footsteps, questioned the very existence of reality and attempted to define it in such a way as it might have originated from a human mind, compartmentalizing it into abstract structures he could understand. He then further claimed that people who thought as he did should be put into power to rule over other people for their own good.

Rationalist Rene Descartes came up with the idea that an evil deceiver might possibly be trying to confuse us about the true reality. This concept of an evil being working as a nemesis of the Creator is rampant throughout Western thought, and is often used to justify all sorts of human behavior. But Descartes is known primarily for his declaration "Cogito, ergo sum', I think therefore I am."

According to Descartes', anything that thinks, exists. Consequently, anything that can confirm the existence of itself to itself is capable of thought; and anything that is capable of thought is alive. But Descartes makes the assumption that there is but one true reality and that man is the only thinking being in that reality.

The empiricist David Hume challenged this and stated that we can never make statements of facts in the world that are necessarily true. This also went contrary to scientific thinking, though scientists often base their work on assumptions, as we shall see later. Jean-Paul Sartre's philosophy, existentialism, did take some scientific advances into account and rejected many of the ideas of earlier philosophers, but still, Sartre too viewed reality solely from the perspective of human existence. And so, even as philosophy has advanced since those days, it has been slow to incorporate the lessons learned in other disciplines.

Western science takes a different approach from philosophy to try to answer the same questions. Science tends to view things in terms of cause and effect. They observe something and then try to determine a rational cause. If the cause fits well enough to not be disproved, they develop a theory to explain things, but in many cases begin to accept it as fact. In some cases, they may even borrow the concept of circular reasoning from philosophy, making a statement that refers to its own assertion in order to prove the assertion.

As an example of the early days of Western science, we might begin with Galileo: Galileo Galilei was a 16th Century Pisan (Italy did not become a unified country until 1861, and Rome did not become a part of it until 1870) who was a physicist, mathematician, astronomer, and philosopher who improved upon the telescope invented in the Netherlands in 1619. Based on his astronomical observations, which include confirming the phases of Venus, and discovering four moons of Jupiter,

Galileo is considered by some to be the "father of modern observational astronomy."

Galileo however, like Socrates, came into opposition with the Church for daring to agree with Copernicus regarding heliocentrism, the radical idea that the Earth revolves around the Sun, and that Man is not the center of the Universe as the Church believed. Galileo was absolutely correct, but for refusing to back away from that, which he knew to be true, Galileo was tried by the Roman Inquisition, declared "vehemently suspect of heresy," forced to recant his scientific findings, and died under house arrest.

In 1590, more than a century before Europeans discovered the existence of the Bering Strait, Jesuit missionary Jose de Acosta theorized that the Indigenous population of the Western Hemisphere must have walked across from Asia. He simply could not fathom that there could have been people in the Western Hemisphere for any period of time without creating the same kind of environmental damage that had happened in Europe. He ruled out the possibility that the Indigenous had arrived on boats, purely because Columbus had required a magnetic compass to stay on course, and the Indigenous people did not have compasses. The problems with that theory are that the alleged Bering Land Bridge, which spanned what is now the Bering Strait, could only have existed during the

Wisconsin glaciation, the last major stage of the Pleistocene epoch beginning 50,000 years ago and ending some 10,000 years ago. Secondly, there is zero archeological evidence that people ever migrated across a land bridge between Asia and the Americas, nor is there evidence of a north to south migration across the continent. Also, there does exist archeological evidence that the hemisphere was inhabited thousands of years before a land bridge might have existed, and that there was a south to north migration. Yet, despite all data to the contrary, de Acosta's theory continues to be taught in American schools as fact well into the 21st Century.

Carl Linnaeus, in 1735, subdivided the human species into four races based on geographic location and skin color: "Europæus albus" (white European), "Americanus rubescens" (red American), "Asiaticus fuscus" (brown Asian) and "Africanus niger" (black African). He detailed what we now would call stereotypical characteristics for each race, based on the ancient concept of humors, four supposed bodily fluids that affect personality and temperament. He later changed the description of Asians' skin tone to "luridus" (yellow). Thomas Jefferson would later use his racial classifications to justify racial hierarchy. Despite the fact that we know today that there is no scientific basis whatsoever to support the concept of race, these classifications are still in use.

The dominance of religion over science, the promotion of pseudo-science, and the teaching of outright lies served to create a society structured in hierarchical classes where the upper class used information to subjugate and control the lower classes. As respected scholar Vine Deloria Jr. once said, "Western civilization, unfortunately, does not link knowledge and morality but rather, it connects knowledge and power and makes them equivalent." This connection between knowledge and power coupled with the influence of religion led to the idea that Nature was there to be harnessed and conquered. The idea of conquest did not stop with plants and animals, but was extended to other humans and to the Earth herself.

On the Western shores of the Atlantic, the Indigenous people of the Western Hemisphere people also were studying this Universe we find ourselves in, attempting to discover the proper way to live and thrive. They developed a highly sophisticated culture centered around the concept of living with the Earth, not on the Earth. Indigenous people accepted the world as it is. Rather than feeling a sense of domination, the people felt a sense of belonging, of being a part of a creation where everything was alive and deserving of respect. They believed, as Descartes did, that anything capable of thought was alive. But they also believed that everything was alive, that everything is conscious at some level. The fact that we cannot detect that consciousness, that a rock or a tree might not communicate that fact to anything or anyone else was irrelevant. All living things were equal in the eyes of the Creator or Great Mystery. An attitude that Man was given dominion and superiority over all (including women) would be considered rude and arrogant.

As Sitting Bull said, "It is through this mysterious power that we too have our being, and we therefore yield to our neighbors, even to our animal neighbors, the same right as ourselves to inhabit this vast land." And so the two-legged beings sought to maintain a balance with the four-legged, the plants, the water animals, the standing people (trees), the rock people, and all of Creation. When it became necessary to take something from Nature, one did it in a respectful manner and was obligated to give something back. Despite living in hundreds of separate nations across the hemisphere, this basic philosophy seems to be one thing the people of the Western Hemisphere had in common.

Indigenous philosophy approached the world, and indeed the universe as a puzzle to be deciphered. Everything is related and nothing is without reason. The fact that one does not understand the reason is just a sign of our ignorance. We are but one of the gears in a colossal machine, and every gear has a function. The challenge is to discover the reason. Indigenous people believe we are here to learn that reason, and while we may at times have a good idea of what the Universe is, the still unanswered question is why. The Indigenous people spent their everyday life not in the accumulation of wealth or material goods, but in the gathering of knowledge about the local environment, the world, and the universe. In today's terminology, we would consider them to be systems engineers.

Indigenous scientists without the benefit of telescopes or any other known instruments calculated the orbits of Venus and Jupiter at least 500 years earlier than Galileo. They also measured the movements of other celestial bodies with a precision that would not be matched until the invention of computers, and even more impressively, made findings based on cycles in the Universe that date back millions of years including the description of a black hole in the center of the Milky Way galaxy. This is something American scientists would discover 3,000 years later, based on gamma ray light from activity estimated to have taken place well over 100,000 years ago. Their knowledge of space/time was used as the basis for entire civilizations, including the geographic layout of cities, the agricultural planting and harvest cycles, and the timing of spiritual ceremonies.

Prior to the European invasion, the Indigenous people of the Western hemisphere had made tremendous scientific breakthroughs in the field of agriculture including the domestication of corn and thousands of varieties of potatoes. Complex calendars were developed as early as 765 CE (Common Era). Entire communities worked in harmony for generations to build pyramids, mounds, cities, and create the Amazon Rain Forest. Woodland forests were managed and periodically burned to promote growth and provide space for wildlife. Conservation was a part of life, a concept that today's people now realize is necessary for the survival of the planet. Who knows what might have been accomplished if the efforts of Indigenous thinkers had not been diverted into a fight for survival over the last 500 years?

Today, Western philosophy has made great strides toward deeper understanding. Mortimer Adler, attempting to prove the existence of God in the 20th Century, speculated that the universe in which we live is only one of many possible universes that might have in fact existed in the past, and might still exist in the future. The universe that we know today is not the only universe that can ever exist in time. Furthermore, there is no reason to think that the natural laws, which govern the universe, are the only possible natural laws. This is the type of thinking that would have been at home among the early Aztecs, the Maya, or the Hopi. But today, organized religions from the Eastern Hemisphere still attempt to control science and philosophy, rejecting any scientific truths that might prove

28

their myths and legends to be metaphoric rather than literal truth.

Modern Western science has incorporated a great deal of Indigenous knowledge, but has its own agenda, using information that can be used to acquire power, and dismissing such things as oral histories if they are contrary to their goals. Representatives of big pharmaceutical corporations have been searching throughout the hemisphere in a quest for ancient cures and herbal remedies that they can "discover," encapsulate, and patent. But the mass production of a cure is not necessarily done in the right way. In one case, a local tribe used a specific plant to cure a disorder. When this became known to a representative of Big Pharma, they bribed local officials, "bought" all the land where the plant grows, and developed an extract that they now sell for hundreds of dollars. The very people who told them about the plant now have to pay to get the drug. The sad irony is that the extract that was developed is not as effective as using the entire raw plant.

Western science has come a long way, but it is now driven by the motivation of profit and power. Consequently, it is still quick to jump to conclusions without all the evidence. We are continually asked to accept the results of complex sciences too arcane to be comprehended by laymen. And they are frequently later proven wrong. They produce drugs that have some limited effect on diseases, but have side effects that are worse than the problems they were designed to correct. They show more interest in producing substances that will reduce symptoms and must be taken for a lifetime, rather than a cure that will eliminate the problem. They publish ideas under the name "Theory," but then teach them as if they were facts. Over the years we have heard of Cold Fusion, Martian canals, Phrenology, Vitamin C as a cure for cancer, and the Static Universe... all later proven wrong.

In thinking of cause and effect, they make the assumption that time is linear, and that there are laws of physics which are immutable. However, more recent research is beginning to hint that these assumptions may be incorrect. Quantum physics has shown us that the laws of physics are more like heuristics; they do not always apply.

Scientists today believe they have discovered the Higgs-Boson particle, an elementary particle in the Standard Model of physics. The existence of this particle would confirm an explanation in quantum physics of how the weak nuclear force, one of the four fundamental forces of nature, works in conjunction with the other three, the strong nuclear force, electromagnetism, and gravity. Its discovery would improve human understanding of our universe by giving us an understanding of how fundamental particles acquire mass. This would help to validate theories and discoveries in particle physics, and open up new ideas of how everything is connected, something Indigenous people have known all along, without scientific proof. But as Albert Einstein once said "There is no logical way to the discovery of these elemental laws. There is only the way of intuition, which is helped by a feeling for the order lying behind the appearance."

As previously mentioned, they have tried to explain the presence of humans in the Western Hemisphere by claiming they must have walked across the Bering Strait: unproven. We have been continually told that there were no people in the Western Hemisphere until fairly recently in geological terms. Is it possible that anthropologists, looking for the type of evidence they would expect to find, based on how people lived in Europe, are misjudging the situation when they are looking for evidence of people who believed in conservation and cleaning up after themselves? The estimates they come up with have to be continually revised as more evidence of human habitation is discovered and they have yet to put together an explanation of why the oldest sites uncovered are at the furthest points in the hemisphere from the Bering Strait. But if they listened to Indigenous people who have an oral history going back thousands of years, many of them will tell you that their people moved from south to north, not the other way around. What then is the reason for perpetuating this fallacy?

The one thing scientists are fairly sure of is that 200 million years ago all the landmasses on the planet were connected as a giant super continent that they call Pangaea. At some point they may discover that there could have been human life on Pangaea before we on Turtle Island drifted away from our African relatives, and there actually may have been a reason why the Mayans were able to describe cosmic events that date back far beyond the estimated time of human life of this planet.

The Indigenous people need to recapture the momentum developed by our ancestors, to write and understand our own history. Most of the history we hear about comes from the conquistador. Our stories and legends are understood to metaphorically represent what actually occurred; but in some cultures, they have re-interpreted their metaphors as documentaries. Then they tell us that our incredible story is a fairy tale and their fairy tales are incredible stories. Perhaps the difference is that, in a culture where the honor of a person's word is valued, the oral tradition is recognized as historical documentation.

It is more common than one might think among Indigenous people, when hearing of the latest scientific "discovery," to see them nodding their heads and saying "We knew that all along. It's about time they discovered it!"

Will we ever decipher the Great Mystery? Who knows?

Perhaps if we ever do, it will simply begin all over again. For now, we need to recognize our place in the Creation, understand that we are ALL related, that everything is alive, and treat everything with respect. We are spiritual beings having a human experience, surrounded by other spiritual beings having different experiences, and our duty today is to restore and save the planet.

I Am Related To The Day

Lois Red Elk

While writing this poem, I was thinking of my mother's Dakota language and how the elements of weather are personalized. We regard wind, thunder or mist as relatives. I am always glad to greet the elements like visiting a family member.

In this evolving evening hour, shades of red from
veins of sinking sun scatter among prairie grasses
    and along the curves of hills tinting all with rosy
    dust. I see silhouettes of Mitakuyepi* move among

gray clouds of Grandfather's breath, the uplifting
of river fog to meet the voices of the coming storm.
    From everywhere they come, the flying ones with
    wings of rain from the west. They come hurriedly

like footsteps along the street. They come rattling
down the side of the house with water drops borrowed
    from the local river. I hear the new songs of young
    thunder, a fresh bird of creator's making for now.

Minute after minute its breath shakes my thoughts
to join the family beings as their roars of joy echo
    in the flash of light glaring from thunderbird's eye.
    Again they come in a sacred way. They come close

with greetings from molecules I wear in my bones, a
light mist I recognize with my skin, a sweet trace of
    blessings signaling silence to leave and pores to open
    for surrender to this other world. They come, these

ancestors, these traditional relatives to wash our minds
and reasonings with a surplus of rotating constellations.
    These songs are translated from the back draft of
    Grandmother, circling our thought-relayed language,

a reminder that we are still receiving wave after wave
of repast in dreams and Godly meditations coming near.
    Something sacred comes this way in hushed sounds
    and calm for the stones to awake and share their birth.

This day I consider mine, the gathering western spirits
have shown themselves, have called attention to what
    we share, in time, and gladdened me with their walk
    and harmony among my prayers, breathing and extent.

*Mitakuyepi means "Relatives" in the D/Lakota language.

Quantum Physics and Good Old Indian Wisdom

Suzanne Zahrt Murphy

This essay is dedicated to Fern Catherine Young Bear, who gave unselfishly as a mentor and who loved well as a relative. And to MariJo Moore, whose patience has provided me with inspiration and understanding. And to Tashunka Wakan, *with love.*

The Sacred Circle

I am a lover of stones from the days of earth. I am a circle, with no beginning, no end.

You live in dance steps called days, and in dream steps called nights.

I live in all, as if in one day. Once in a while you see me.

Sometimes you lose me, sometimes you reject me, and always I see you.

Sometimes you forsake one another, and fall. Your tears fall on me, and the greenness of forgiveness comes. I see you, in your fire, and in your wholeness. I watch as you live in the voice of the whirlwind, and in the appearance of darkness. I wait until you find yourself again.

And you will. Remember your *real* self, the one that is connected to everything else, and you remember me. Remember one another, and you remember me.

For all is one. The ancients knew this, the old ones, my relatives. [1]

ONE: SCIENCE

Science and ancient ideas have long been at odds with one another. But science, using the name *quantum physics*, seems to be making friends with good old Indian wisdom. (In the discourse below, the author adds bold italics.)

What is quantum physics? On the Internet the following definition is found: "From a mathematical point of view, what really distinguishes quantum mechanics from its classical predecessors is that states and quantities...form families with a more interesting network of **relations** among their members..." [2]

Well, how does this work? Some background can be found in the book, *Uncommon Wisdom* by Fritjof Capra. Capra came to this country to study particle physics in the sixties, working as a theoretical physicist. During the course of his work through the seventies, he soon found that discoveries realized by quantum physics could cause "revolutionary" ways of looking at the world, from the idea of "building blocks" and structure, to one of a vast and interconnecting web in which relationship and creativity are the key factors:

"Ultimately, as I understand it, at least in the physical world, trees, chairs and people are, underneath it all, the same, with the same predisposition to form 'systems,' depending on what is observing it. And the same light surrounds all things..." [3] While working with the principles of quantum physics, Capra simultaneously began to study Taoism, and realized this science was related to ancient wisdom. He wrote a book called *The Tao of Physics* about his findings, and in the subsequent book, *Uncommon Wisdom*, he lamented a corruption of science into *scientism:*

"Galileo said, 'Whatever cannot be measured and quantified is not scientific'; and in post-Galilean science this came to mean 'What cannot be quantified is not real.' This has been the most profound corruption from the Greek view of nature as *physis*, which is **alive, always in transformation and not divorced from us**." [4]

According to Capra, science, until quantum physics seemed to believe that if you don't see it, it doesn't exist. The new quantum physics, was a "...view of living organisms as self-organizing systems." Biological forms (matter), Capra defined were "*manifestations* of underlying processes."

Now most of us will be a little boggled by these definitions and abstracts. Capra tried to put his ideas into plain language by making a film. In the movie, "Mindwalk," in which the screenplay is taken from Capra's book *Turning Point,* a physicist tries to explain particle physics to two laymen, a poet and a United States senator:

"The old way of thinking was from the philosopher Descartes, who theorized that the world is made up of a system of 'building blocks,' structured like a sturdy machine...he felt that you could take apart the pieces of all things and put them all back together." [5] "But," the physicist tells them, "particle physics brought about a crisis in scientific perception, because, at the subatomic level, matter is found to have no specific place...the only thing that can be predicted are certain properties." [6] She adds that a nucleus cannot be foretold for certain, and that matter doesn't exist in definite places, but shows tendencies... probabilities:

"Scientists can't say it is in a definite place or has a path; can't say for sure if it moves or stays still...therefore, there are only 'probability patterns, (of, say, stone) which arrange themselves... in 'patterns of interconnections'...*the essence of matter lies in relationships*." [7]

Capra uses the film to promote ideas of responsibility and relationship - consciousness - to life, the planet, and each other.

Could life and its "living systems of a certain complexity" have an orchestration? Says Capra: "The Mystical view...is based on **direct experience**...The system view...the conventional scientific view [is] that consciousness is a property...of living systems of a certain complexity." [8] [Human beings vs. animals or rocks author]

"On the other hand, the biological structures of these systems are manifestations of underlying processes. What processes? Well, the **processes of self-organization**, which we have identified as mental processes. If we extend this way of thinking to the universe as a whole, it is not too far-fetched to assume that all its structures - from subatomic particles to galaxies and from bacteria to human beings - are manifestations of the universal dynamics of self-organization, which means of **the cosmic mind**. And this, more or less, is the mystical view." [9]

Self-organization? Cosmic mind? Capra decided to study Asian philosophies, specifically Taoism, and found a correlation to his view of Mysticism. An example of Taoist thought can be seen in the following two quotes by Lao Tzu: "Thirty spokes share one hub." [10] "As a thing, the way is Shadowy, indistinct." [11]

Sound familiar? Soon Capra recognized that the concept of *Chi*, in Chinese medicine, described what scientists were beginning to understand: "*Chi* is not a substance, nor does it have the purely quantitative meaning of our scientific concept of energy. It is used in Chinese medicine in a very subtle way to describe the various **patterns of flow and fluctuation** in the human organism...*Chi*...seems to represent the principle of flow...which, in the Chinese view, is always *cyclical*." [12]

Ah! Indigenous peoples all over the world have not only known about our connectedness, and the cycles of life, but also about consciousness, and that of higher consciousness - **the cosmic mind,** which some call by different names: Mystery, Creator, God, Spirit, and so on - for thousands of years.

Western psychology still wants to separate mind from spirit, or to divide awareness into categories such as "the soul," and "the spirit," as if they were different. Indigenous wisdom does not do this, but has practiced holistic awareness from antiquity.

Further, the wisdom is NOT, as Western thought would have us think, metaphor, but rather an expression about **a living thing not divorced from us**. Life is the self-organizing perpetuation of itself, and everything is part of it.

TWO: INDIAN WISDOM

Let's look again at Mysticism, (defined as "direct experience" by Capra). The late Vine Deloria Jr., renowned American Indian scholar and author, understood Mysticism and particle physics very well. In his book, *The World We Used to Live in, Remembering the Powers of the Medicine* Men, he wrote about examples of the direct experience of Medicine people (or Holy ones) and of those who sought vision. Of scientific theory, he said:

"Time and space were the defining concepts of Western philosophical tradition from the Greek atomists until the mid-twentieth century, when we were able to split the atom and show that the Einstein formula $E=MC2$ described the substance of the universe. These concepts were believed to represent absolute entities in the composition of the universe... they represented a structured universe and were dependable in that they always formed the context within which everything else happened.

"With the discoveries in subatomic physics, we learned that they merged together and became useless when describing miniscule atomic events. Today, they are regarded as flexible concepts, useful in a human-sized world, but increasingly mysterious at macro and micro levels of inquiry." [13]

As for consciousness, Deloria states, "There seems to be a reasonable number of Western scientists and thinkers who subscribe to the idea that the ultimate constituent of the universe is mind, or mind-stuff...tribal peoples observed the world around them and quickly concluded that it represented *an energetic mind ungirding the physical world, its motions, and provided energy and life in everything that existed...”*[14]

Our ancestors already knew, through prayer and a "direct experience," that the world is **alive, always in transformation, and not divorced from us**. More importantly, they recognized responsibility to the world.

Traditions were a result of the experiences, visions and dreams of those who lived in direct communication with the all. No matter which people or place one comes from, there are stories, traditions, and ceremonies to explain the importance of relatedness and of the circular concept of space and time. In the following quotes from various Indigenous people, the in-depth wisdom concerning these beliefs is revealed:

"...the ultimate aim of Dakota life, stripped of accessories, was quite simple: One must obey kinship rules; one must be a good relative...In   the last analysis, every other consideration was secondary - property, personal   ambition, glory, good times, life itself...." Ella Deloria. [15]

"You take something of yourself and give it free. You take a part of yourself and do so because you believe you are connected to everything else. You become aware of yourself as a part of everything. You suffer momentarily so that someone else will not   have to." Unknown Winnebago [16]

"You have noticed that everything an Indian does is in a circle, and   that is because the Power of the World always works in circles, and   everything tries to be round..." Black Elk [17]

"*Awi Usdi*, Little Deer

Ginitsi Selu

Corn, Mother of Us all

in perfect balance

in perfect union..." [18] Marilou Awiakta

"The major difference between American Indian views of the physical world and Western science lies in the premise accepted by Indians and rejected by scientists: **the world in which we live is alive**." Vine Deloria Jr. [19]

"Indians came to understand that all things were related..." Vine Deloria Jr. [20]

"I know that our people possessed remarkable powers of concentration and abstraction, and I sometimes fancy that such nearness to nature ...keeps the spirit sensitive to impressions not commonly felt, and in touch with the unseen powers." Ohiyesa [21]

When particle physics gained prominence, suddenly relationships could be said to exist. "Legitimacy" in the world of Western Science was given to what was **already** legitimate in the eyes of the Indigenous: the entire world is alive. With the understanding of the physical world as being part of "all things," tribes (peoples) developed traditions and practices that were part of their lives that included the seen and the unseen, animals, rocks, plants, all parts of creation.

Being part of a tribe or a people helps us to understand our part in this web of "fluctuation and flow." As Ella Deloria wrote, "... relationships can be based on patterns of thought and behavior and be equally as binding as relationships of blood." [22]

Being part of the circle, part of the "web," means that you had to pay attention to your relationship to others, to your "kinship." Would that we, in secular society, remembered this. Part of growing up in what my dear friend the late elder Fern Young Bear (Standing Rock Hunkpapa) called "the dominant society," creates a terrible sense of isolation, even exile. With individualism, a lack of responsibility is supposed. The idea of hierarchy, upon which the scientific classification system is arranged, echoing in kingdoms and governments, creates an imbalance. Many modern-day relationships are *Koyaanisqatsi*, a Hopi word meaning "life out of balance."

In contrast, tribal societies placed the group (tribe, or nation) kinship first, the individual, last. Young Bear stated, "What is so different between Indians and non-Indians is that we are members of a tribe, even if we do not always show it." [23] And then she goes on to explain: "Our 'hierarchy,' if one must think in those terms, places the tribe at the top, then the clan, extended family, natural family, chosen family, and the individual at the bottom. This does not mean that we have low self-esteem.

It means the opposite, that we value the well-being of the people and our psychology and philosophy is all-inclusive, not segregated into pieces of the whole of our lives." [24]

Crisis management was not new to Indians. Our peoples inhabited this land and used the wisdom that it taught through the directions, the wind, the colors of life, and the other beings. And all of this knowledge remains in our blood as Cherokee writer MariJo Moore reminds us: "Somewhere in the deepest recesses of your heart, you can find your interconnectedness to the crows, trees, deserts, moon and rivers." [25] The people also knew how to deal with those who were not respectful of the important interconnectedness of the universe. The late Wilma Mankiller, former chief of the Cherokee Nation, wrote: "Among the many revered Cherokee formulas, there is one for the treatment of ordeal diseases... the disease is often sent to someone by a friend or even a parent, to test the afflicted person's endurance and knowledge of counter spells. The prayer is addressed to the Black, Red, Blue, and White ravens, which are each in turn declared to have put the disease in to a crevice in *Sanigilagi* - the Cherokee name of Whiteside Mountain, at the head of Tuckaseegee River, in North Carolina. The term is used figuratively for any high precipitous mountain. The word *adawehi*, which is used several times in the formula, refers to a magician or supernatural being...." [26]

The strengths taught by the ancestors who understood the relationships of all things have not been lost. Mankiller, like many modern-day Indians, knew that the wisdom would sustain her: "I drew on the strength of my ancestors and of present-day Cherokee medicine people, and on my own internal resolve to remove all negative factors from my life so I could focus on healing." [27] Being of good mind and not allowing negative thoughts can be said to be "good medicine."

The afore-mentioned Fern Catherine Young Bear once told this author to say "let nothing negative enter here," whether it be the bad thoughts or jealousy of another, or one's own negative thoughts. She knew that thoughts are the energy that produces effect.

Young Bear also believed that our actions are important. The elder, who took her spirit journey in 2005, often made quilts in which she "put love and prayers in every stitch." She stated, "The *Ahani* (old or ancient) way is a humble way: the young helped the old, the strong helped the weak and vulnerable. No one shamed another, even if someone was wrong. One did not try to gain personal admiration over it. We tried not to hurt someone's feelings. Helping another to save face kept everyone respectful." [28]

We all have responsibility to the planet and to each other. In his book *Uncommon Wisdom,* Capra took the premises of particle physics and "connected the dots" to ideas about our responsibility to life. Systems, including economics to the environment are included in this idea. From there he recognized that we have responsibility to remember our inter-connectedness. The ancient ones already knew this. For those of us who must strain to understand physics (this author included), reading Indian wisdom and spending time with elders can provide richness and understanding concerning the never-ending circle of life.

On a personal note, my great grandmother was a mid-wife who grew herbal medicines. I never knew her well enough to learn from her, a yearning that causes me great sadness. When I began my journey to re-connect with my heritage (*Tsalagi/* Cherokee, plus German, Scot and Swede) I had a dream, a "direct experience."

In the dream, I was looking out across a river. Seven men, wearing braids and feathers on their heads, dressed in buckskin leggings, rowed across the river in a canoe. They greeted me with smiles and waved and sang to me. Then a series of dreams about being Indian came to me, one after another. A most profound one included a native man and woman who came with a beautiful beaded jacket. They held it up to me; it was so very beautiful, I could not stop looking at it. They beckoned to me to wear it. I put it on, and it fit perfectly. One event after another occurred which led me to meet people who have taught me how to remember who I am.

I was impatient, as is one who is raised in dominant society. I had to learn to trust. Young Bear reminded me that being part of the connected world is not something that comes and goes; it is a commitment. By knowing her and by keeping in communication with MariJo Moore, my life has been enriched a thousand fold. Instead of striving to "become" I have realized that I am already whole, and that life tests us but we are given the strength to live. "You have to believe," Young Bear told me. And I do.

All My Relations.

1 Murphy, Suzanne Zahrt, unpublished poem ©2008
2 Internet: Wikipedia; 4/14/07: *Stanford Encyclopedia of Philosophy* (First Published November 2000).
3 Capra, Fritjof. *Uncommon Wisdom: Conversations with Remarkable People.* New York: Bantam Books, 1988. 133.
4 Ibid. 137
5 "Mindwalk movie. 1990. Bernt Capra (story), Floyd Byars screenplay from the book *Turning Point* by Fritjof Capra.
6 Ibid.
7 Ibid.
8 Capra, Fritjof. *Uncommon Wisdom: Conversations with Remarkable People.* New York: Bantam Books, 1988. 135.
9 Ibid. 136
10 Lau, DC, Editor. *Lao Tzu, Tao Te Ching. New York:* Penguin Books, 1963, 15.
11 Ibid. 26
12 Capra, Fritjof. *Uncommon Wisdom: Conversations with*

Remarkable People. New York: Bantam Books, 1988, 160

13 Deloria, Vine Jr. *The World We Used to Live In: Remembering the Powers of the Medicine Men.* Golden, CO: Fulcrum Publishing, 2006, 201-202

14 Ibid. 195-197

15 Deloria, Ella. *Waterlily.* Lincoln, NE: University of Nebraska Press, 1988, Preface/X

16 Hill, Norbert S. (Oneida) Editor. Unknown Winnebago. *Words of Power, Voices from Indian America.* Golden, CO: Fulcrum Publishing, 1999. 37

17 Niehardt, John G. *Black Elk Speaks.* Lincoln, NE: University of Nebraska Press, 1932. Preface

18 Awiakta, Marilou. *Selu: Seeking the Corn Mother's Wisdom.* Golden, CO: Fulcrum Publishing, 1993, 326

19 Deloria, Vine Jr. *Red Earth, White Lies.* Golden, CO: Fulcrum Publishing, 1997, 40

20 Ibid. 41

21 Hill, Norbert S. (Oneida) Editor. Ohiyesa - Dr. Charles Eastman. *Words of Power, Voices from Indian America.* Golden, CO: Fulcrum Publishing, 1999, 4

22 Deloria, Ella. *Waterlily.* Lincoln, NE: University of Nebraska Press, 1988, Preface/XII

23 Young Bear, Fern Catherine. *Ahani: The Ways of Long Ago and Today.* Standing Rock, ND: Self-published, 2005, 6

24 Ibid. 9

25 Moore, MariJo. *Desert Quotes.* Candler, NC: rENEGADE pLANETS pUBLISHING, 2000, no page numbers in booklet

26 Mankiller, Wilma and Michael Wallace *Mankiller A Chief and Her People An Autobiography.* NY: St. Martin's Press, 1993, 231

27 Ibid. 228

28 Young Bear, Fern Catherine. *Ahani: The Ways of Long Ago and Today.* Standing Rock, ND: Self-published, 2005,3

Quantum Lakota

Amy Krout-Horn

The eagle feather appeared one summer afternoon as the tide flowed out and the shifting breeze flowed in, and as the gulls and terns rested on the bone-white beach, just beyond the fringe of the sea and the sand's fusion.

It occurred as I had knelt chest deep in the sway of slow rolling surf, body and mind moving with the rhythm of the waves. Gabriel sat beside me, his gaze flitting from the flashes of silver fish to the sun shafts that connected the liquid world with the world of air. On its surface, the water sparkled in a mystical way; in the way spirits manifest themselves inside the lodge during *Inipi*, the purification ceremony. In that moment, we, too, existed in a state of ceremonial consciousness, the state in which the universe's infinite possibilities reveal themselves, falling from the hidden folds of another layer of reality, into our physical plain. Gabriel blinked at the turquoise water, looked at the sky, and then dropped his eyes back to the Gulf of Mexico. Whispering, he shifted us from our shared silence.

"Is that…?"

He swam towards an object floating where, not longer than a breath before, nothing, accept the miles of blue sea, had been visible. Lifting it gently from the placid surface, he walked the few strides back to me. I emerged from the water, intrigue rising, as anticipatory tingles traveled across my skin.

"Look," he said, and I shook the water free from my hands.

More than a decade ago, not long after I had survived my twenty-first winter, diabetes stole my sight, starting with shape, then taking the light, and concluding its crime with the removal of my infected eyes. But as I felt the wing feather brushing my palms, I knew that the vision of the eye was not requisite. Its flawless symmetry and the unexpected dry sensation I found when I ran my fingertips along the quill, spoke of its beauty, its magic, and its power. The longer I touched this holy entity, the deeper, the wider, the greater, the feeling of wholeness grew, until I caressed more than an eagle feather. I caressed the eagle, the sky, the stars, and the universe.

The shell presented itself in the same waters, in a different, but no less mysterious manner. On our return to Passagrille, Gabriel and I noticed that the circle had not yet vanished. He had drawn it in the sand many days earlier, when we had come to the beach at the dawn of the summer solstice, when first light filtered through sable palms and sea oats, when we had stepped inside the center and smoked the *chanunpa*, sacred pipe, acknowledging the birth of a new season, acknowledging the beginning of our life together. In the nights following the ceremony, a sea turtle had visited the shore, selecting the interior of the round outline to build a nest for her eggs. And I found great peace in knowing that our circle now served another very special purpose.

Clasping hands, we entered the water and I waited, as he let go, dove in, and swam out to the sand bar. When he reached it, he called to me that it was all right to follow; I plunged beneath the breakers, breeched the surface, then swam a slow crawl towards the sound of his voice. Where the plateau had formed, the water lapped, very warm and shallow over the fine sand and blue crabs scurried clear of our shuffling feet. Gabriel took my hand again and we splashed along, up to our ankles until the sand began its gradual downwards slope towards a point where it dropped into the darker, deeper ocean. Here, we stopped and stretched out, Gabriel leaning on his side, propped on one elbow. I lay on my stomach, the prone position evoking sweet memories of a mid-western childhood. The temperate water washed away layers of time until the Tree Popping Moon, with its spiraling tempests of snow and biting icy wind, returned. But winter's frigid teeth could not clutch me, for I had closed my eyes and swam on my round little belly, through the magical sea in my grandparent's old claw foot tub. I kicked and stroked passed the octopus washcloth and the Ivory soap shark until the water turned cool and Grandma scooped me up in her arms, wrapping me in fluffy towels.

As I drifted between the past and the present, Gabriel collected small scallop, conch, and clamshells and placed them one by one, adorning my bare shoulders. Tucking a sliver of glittering abalone in the strands of my hair, he told the story of White Shell Woman, the wife of the Sun. I let my hands sink into the soft sand and as it surrounded my wrists, my palm pressed against something smooth and solid. Without thinking, I closed my fingers around it and felt a strange quiver, not like the squirm of a captured creature, but more like a flowing energy current, and I did not want to let go. I loosened it from the sand and brought it above the water, opening my fist and showing it to Gabriel. Opening and closing my fingers around it again, he commented on how its shape and size fit perfectly in my hand. I asked what he thought it might be.

"It's a fossilized clam."

The petrified shell pulsed, a stone heart beating an ancient song of change, of transformation, of eons. *Time,* I thought and grasped the relic more tightly, *I am touching time.*

In the years since love transported me from Minnesota and transplanted me in Florida, other unexplained items have materialized, as well. We live in a small bungalow, on an island not far from the mouth of Tampa Bay, not far from where, armed with arrows of fire, *Calusa* warriors defeated Spanish invaders, sinking their galleons beneath the present day shadows of the Sunshine Skyway Bridge. Behind the house, Gabriel has crafted a medicine wheel, using the large stones that he carried from North Carolina many years ago. Very soon after the grandfathers were arranged in their circle, the other stones began to arrive, showing up on closet shelves, in the sandy front yard, and at the back of drawers. Two appeared one night as we slept, Gabriel discovering them beside the pipe bundle when he awoke. Smooth round stones kept cropping up; some like small black beans, others, the size of a red grape, some with the shape and dimensions of a snake's egg, the largest, as big as a cantaloupe.

One evening, as Gabriel sat on the porch, quietly watching the stars glimmering against the dark of a new moon, he felt something hard under the sole of his foot. Reaching beneath the chair, he withdrew another stone, elliptical and the color of charcoal. He rotated it, recognizing the now familiar texture, but as he held it up in the starlight, he saw something unique. In the center of one side, a line of pale mineral swirled through it, creating a spiral, a whirlwind of power descending into and ascending out from the stone's hidden universe.

In the kitchen, I daydreamed to the song of cicadas rising and falling outside the screen door, while I stood with a wooden spoon at the stove, stirring chicken stew in slow, easy circles. Gabriel came in and put the stone in my free hand. I set the spoon down and he traced my index finger along the spiral. Like the eagle feather and the clamshell, it emitted something mystical, something beautiful. It contained the message of all things too magnificent and all things too minute for the mind to comprehend.

And yet, a feeling persisted, a feeling of connectiveness between everything seen and unseen, weaving together everything that is known with everything that is unknown.

Like a holy trinity of our time-honored native spirituality, the feather, the shell, and the stone remind me of the wisdom of my ancestors, the ancient wisdom that precedes modern quantum physics by thousands of years. Yet, although it has often been considered a dangerous enemy of Christian, Judaic, and Islamic ideologies, scientific theory has begun to align with traditional indigenous beliefs. Terminology differs, but western science cannot disguise the old tribal teachings behind a complicated conceptual curtain woven with new semantics. Innovative theoretical physicists describe our universe as a "net". We, as native people, speak of the "web". They acknowledge that all matter within the universe has an interconnected relationship. By speaking the words *mitaku oyasin*, I, like generations of Lakota, honor "all our relations," and we remember the sacred hoops within the one great hoop that the Oglala holy man, Black Elk, witnessed through his vision.

When their calculations do not deliver the solution to the unanswerable question and their theories fall short of explaining the force that weaves the cosmos into one living entity, such words as "incompleteness" and "indeterminable variable" pop up. Some of the scientific community's most brilliant icons have even reverted to the notion that their anthropomorphic god is keeping himself amused with a divine dice game. But we, who have chosen not to relinquish our belief in ancient wisdom, know of what they speak. We have always known. We do not assign a gender or search for it through the lenses of a microscope, a telescope, or at the end of a string of numbers. We live within it and it lives within us. For a Lakota whose spirit still cradles the precious philosophical wisdom of the ancestors, we say *Wakan Tanka*, Great Mystery.

As I cup the round stone in my hand, I contemplate what humans will do with the ideas that science has introduced. Will they realize the negative impact their actions are inflicting upon all the nations; the two-legged, four-legged, winged, water beings, insect peoples, tree and plant nations? Will they feel the pain of our mother, the Earth? Will they stop raping her for oil, coal, uranium, gold, and diamonds? Can love and respect cure these addictions?

I draw the shell from the medicine bag. Will Dr. Masaru Emoto's experiments with the emotions of water change their attitudes? Will the ones who make and the ones who break environmental policies hear the messages? How many more whales must die of cancer? How many more outbreaks of deadly red tide will ravage the oceans? How many more fish, contaminated with mercury, will be eaten?

Then, I slide the shell back into the leather pouch, suspending it from a hook on the wall beside the window and I bring the eagle feather from its place on the shelf above. As the sky opens and rain begins to fall, I touch the feather to my forehead, needing thoughts to enter, thoughts that will turn into written words. For a long time, images and ideas fly around inside my head, ideas about quarks and sub-atomic particles and light waves. But rain splashes the palm fronds and the wind chime sways back and forth in the oak tree until thought fades away. All the empirical and theoretical evidence cannot evolve the spirit if the learners do not live in accordance with the principles they have learned. I take the feather from against my head and hold it over my heart. The feeling comes. The feeling carries the words. I speak the words aloud.

"*Wakan Tanka* is in everything. Everything is in *Wakan Tanka*."

The Nature of the Universe

Jack D. Forbes

The cosmic visions of Indigenous peoples are significantly diverse. Each nation and community has its own unique traditions. Still, several characteristics stand out. First, it is common to envision the creative process of the universe as a form of thought or mental process. Second, it is common to have a source of creation that is plural; either because several entities participate in creation or because the process as it unfolds includes many sacred actors stemming from a First Principle (Father/Mother or Grandfather/Grandmother). Third, the agents of creation are seldom pictured as human, but are depicted instead as "wakan" (holy), or animal-like (coyote, raven, great white hare, etc.), or as forces of nature (such as wind/breath). Perhaps the most important aspect of indigenous cosmic visions is the conception of creation as a living process, resulting in a living universe in which a kinship exists between all things. Thus the Creators are our family, our Grandparents or Parents, and all of their creations are children who, of necessity, are also our relations.

Algonkian tongues, Lenápe for one,
    call the Creator *Kiche Manito* or *Ketanitowit*,
    Meaning the Great One Who Exceeds or the
    Great Exceeding Power
    And wonder we must if our Universe arose from the Great
    Compression or from a mysterious birthing of atoms in
    space, as Hoyle believed.

The Universe, is it a sphere,
    is it limited in extent or infinite in time and space,
    or will it eventually slow down, collapse, and fall in on itself,
    back down to a single point?

Some physicists have told us of a sphere-like Universe
    which expands in time from First Movement but how can
    one create a sphere, a ball-shape, from a single point
    unless the different galaxies (as they say) have traveled
    very different distances?

Others speak of "open universe" models where the
    galaxies spread apart on a layer of space which
    is infinite horizontally and expansion continues
    laterally forever
    and ever on that rather thin sheet of space.

Some scientists tell tales
　　of a boundless *Wemi Tali* (the All Where, Everywhere)
　　obeying the rules of spherical geometry,
　　but without being a sphere, since spheres,
　　from Greek *sphaira*,
　　are, like all balls, bounded, with a shape, with
　　surface frontiers.

And every sphere is, like a globe,
　　ended, bordered, because to be non-bordered
　　is to be not a ball
　　not a sphere but rather a shape-less indescribable
　　no-thing.

Others tell tales in which our Universe could be
　　envisioned as a balloon
　　gradually being blown up with galaxies being carried
　　farther apart as they adhere to the surface of the balloon.

Pues bien, but does such an analogy
　　really tell us anything since the galaxies are
　　not glued to the surface of a balloon?
　　indeed, some physicists even deny the existence of a skin,
　　a border, an outside; thus how can there be a surface?

Space, in total, is said to be finite
    but what can that mean?
    Finite means "fin", finished, limited, bordered,
    and does not the logic of our mind argue that no end
    can exist without the beginning of something else?

Without a border, a front,
    something new, an out there, a beyond,
    there is no expansion possible, *keeche* (really)?

The nature of the Universe, of space,
    is to be curved it is said,
    which reminds us of the sacredness of circles
    among our American nations
    a reflection
    of all life, it is said.

Of the Universe, I have written:
    "…we are indeed, its vibrating
    glowing receptors…
    for we, the observers…
    are its eyes and ears…

We and all the animals and
   living things
   we complete the world…

If the world be a drum
   we are its taut skin
   vibrating
   with its messages…"

"The Nature of the Universe" is excerpted from *What is Space? : consciousness, voids, and universes*, Kahonkok Press Jack D. Forbes, © 2001. The intro is excerpted from an essay titled Indigenous Americans: Spirituality and Ecos © Jack D. Forbes, 2005. Both printed here with permission (given in 2006) of the late author.

Part Two

Cosmologies of Indigenous Medicine, Ceremonialism, and Perspectives Therefore

Medicine comes in the form of thought, spiritual transformation, inner workings of emotions, and soul retrievals. Some medicine people have powers that can affect weather and climate, which can positively affect food production. Some medicine is humor—laughter being one of our most sacred forms of survival. Some medicine uses herbal remedies. Regardless, Indigenous medicine is a tool of seeking balance: physical, spiritual, emotional, and relationship wise.

Ceremony, in Indigenous perspective, is a necessary act to obtain or regain balance with the universe. The purpose of ceremony is to integrate: to unite one with all of humankind as well as the realm of the ancestors, to blend one with all of creation. This allows one to raise consciousness and shed the idea of individuality, of separation. Ceremony brings one into balance with all there is and renews relationships with cyclical time, allowing entrance in to sacred space. Each ceremony has its own special purpose. Of course, the purposes vary from group to group, from nation to nation. Nevertheless, all ceremony brings one to the realization there is no separation from anything or any one, provides great illumination, and gives one perception of a cosmic relationship.

Green Corn

John D. Berry

Time: We are caught behind the watch face of the Euro-immigrant trap of linear time in our work a day world. However our ceremonial cycles have adapted to deal with that, those cycles are still there and based on worldly cycles. We participate in seasonal time, the cycle of lunar time, the time of the natural world. We are not above it, nor pretended masters of it, or separated from it. Past is present and future, the time of no time and all time. We participate in ceremony with all those who have done so before, for all of those now who cannot for whatever reason, and for all of those to come - there is no separation. Time out of mind, reaching back beyond current memory, to memory in the blood, our very DNA reaching back and forward.

> Dawn's light.
>
> Prayers on the winds.
>
> The people gather, laughing.
>
> Sun's light.
>
> Smoke rising from the ground's fire.

The people gather in earth circle, for healing.

First the children, then the women, finally,

only the men.

Moon rises,

all gather to eat.

Then the call comes.

Shells shake, the drum speaks,

the people move in stomp together.

Time is now, and time is then,

stepping timeless, in earth circle.

Sun dims, night falls,

our fires burn

mirroring Creator's in timeless circles.

Let the people move together, let them be well.

May it always be so.

Lakota Identity

Sidney Cook Bad Moccasin, III

Hau Mitakuyepi. I would first like to introduce myself; my name is Wounspe Okhuwa, which means Pursues Knowledge. I am of the Wazhazha Clan. On my maternal side of the family I descend from Chief Quick Bear and belong to the Black Pipe and Wazhazha People clans of the Pine Ridge and Rosebud Sioux Tribes. On my paternal side, I descend from Chief Crawler's son, Chief Eagle Shield of Little Eagle, SD, located on the Standing Rock Sioux Reservation.

Hau Mitakuyepi. We must remember as Lakota people that these ceremonies that were handed down to us through the generations are not obligations, they are responsibilities for cultural continuity, and it is our law to ensure that these ceremonies continue, or shame our ancestors by not performing them. These Holy Rites are not options; instead they are mandatory responsibilities as parents and adults, and members of the beautiful Lakota "Sioux" Nation. We do not integrate any other religious cult or organization into our Seven Holy Rites brought to us Lakota people by Pte San Win, White Buffalo Calf Woman. Christian/Catholic dogmas are not mixed into our ceremonies out of the respect we hold for our own original teachings and for other cultures and their beliefs.

This story belongs to my *Tiyospaye* (extended family), the Bad Moccasin and Sharp Butte extended families of South Dakota. Every Lakota and Dakota family unit has its own rich stories of emergence related to our identity as Lakota people. Everyone must remember that there are specific sequences and specific songs that must be sung during the performance of these ceremonies. My only reason for sharing this story is to enrich the lives of my people because many of our families have lost vital information due to the recent conflicts of our past and the oppression and genocide that tried to crush and eradicate our traditional way of life as Lakota people.

Recently, I have been revisiting my thoughts and memories of the stories that were shared with me by my late maternal grandfather, Mr. William Howard Sharp Butte, Sr., who belonged to the Quick Bear Clan and Black Pipe District on the Rosebud Lakota reservation in South Dakota. My grandfather and I would sit at his dinner table in respectful silence while enjoying our coffee before our usual cruise to visit our *Tiyospaye*. On one bright and beautiful morning I noticed a mark on my grandfather's right arm, just hidden under his Black Hills gold watch. It was a blue mark, a symbol, an old design. This is what my story is based on…that mark on his skin, a tattoo.

I decided to document my memories and pass a small

portion of this information on to my family, friends, and those intrigued by my illustrious, and rich Lakota culture and way of living before I make my journey back home to tell my grandfathers about my travels and experiences on this Sacred Earth. I have decided to include this story in print form for documentation prosperity; it's a story that is passed down through the generations in my family by oral storytelling since the beginning of time. It seems as though most Lakota families have lost their knowledge and wisdom—an unfortunate and true fact. I hope that message reaches the eyes and ears of the youth in my communities.

I begin with the human spirit and its existence. My grandfather told me that before we are born, before our mothers give birth to us physically, our spirit lies in the South Direction. In this holy place, considered very sacred, is where all our ancestors and relatives reside. We Lakota people call this place *Ite Okagata,* "The Place Where the Spirit Faces Collect." It is referred to as *Wichoni,* or "The Source of Life," or *Masteyata* (The place of constant warmth and goodness). When our cherished Lakota elders speak during ceremonies, they mention this special place. The One Grandfather, the Creator lies in the deepest depths beyond the clouds and sky, beyond the stars. Referred in Lakota as "That Which Moves Things" or "The Power of Motion," which truly is *Wakan Tanka* (The Great Mystery) resides there in *Wichoni.*

As spirits before human birth, we approached the Creator and our grandfathers (as my grandfather explained to me, there are exactly 16 Grandfathers in *Wichoni*). As we stood before them, we offered our Grandfathers *chanshasha* (red willow bark/red dogwood) that is placed inside a *Channunupa* (Sacred Pipe) and asked permission and blessings to journey to earth. This sacred act is called *Opagipi* (a spiritual contract). This particular spiritual agreement or contract cannot be broken or undone. It is said that if we adhere to our visions and our dreams and complete our promises here on earth, we will go directly back to the Creator, back to the farthest deepest depths beyond the stars. There at that place, the ancient spirits reside, they say. It is at this sacred and holy place where our Grandfather Spirits come to help when we call them into our healing ceremonies: the *Inipi, Lowanpi* and *Yuwipi.*

Once The Grandfathers have accepted our offerings, listened to our proposals, and heard our pleas, they give their blessings by bestowing us with the tools necessary—their wisdom and knowledge. They allow us to make our journey to earth and appoint us four spirit guides or spirit helpers. As we leave their presence, *Tunkasila* (the One Grandfather) calls our Lakota spirit name out into the eternal abyss throughout the universe four times to ensure that our spirits will be strong enough to sustain a healthy life as a child on this earth.

Before we enter our physical body, we first choose our parents, it is said. After we have chosen our parents, and after conception, we enter this world and our new body. As Lakota people, our spirit walks up *Wanagi Txachanku* (Road of the Spirits), also known as the Red Road or Milky Way; this is one concept the Lakota shared with the world. When we have reached the Big Dipper or what we Lakota call *Wicaki Yuhapi* (The Stretcher), we descend down a path worn deep into the handle of the Big Dipper and enter this world through the center of the Dipper, between the four stars.

My grandfather told me that at one time there lived a woman's spirit at the center of those four stars in the Big Dipper; her name is *Wichahpi To Winyan* (Lady Blue Star). She is a spirit who helps the midwives during child labor and birth. The midwives pray to her for assistance and a safe and healthy birth for both mother and child. Blue Star Woman used to come to earth before any European ever stepped onto our continent. A relative of mine recently told me that Blue Star Woman would come down from the middle of the Big Dipper to visit, as she would notice our campfires glowing in our homes. She left for good as the people were beginning to ignore her teachings; they didn't want to listen any longer. So it is said she went back to the Big Dipper and there the people saw the Blue Star explode and blue lights were seen going out all over the night sky.

So, we have very vital reasons for being on this earth. We have to be careful with our choices and decisions, to be responsibly accountable for our actions and behavior, and how we respect and treat our relatives and ourselves. We have an identity as Lakota-Dakota people; this identity is our culture, language, songs, stories and ceremonies, The Seven Holy Rites, **or** Seven Sacred Gifts brought to us by our Grandmother *Pte San Win* (White Buffalo Calf Lady).

When a child is first born, the midwives wash him or her with water and sage as a welcome blessing. After being united with the birth mother for four whole days and nights, the Lakota infant is sung over by a Holy Man on the fifth morning. The ceremony consists of having the proper instruments: *wasna* (dried cornmeal/chokecherry and dried meat mixture), a bowl of water, and *wojapi* (chokecherry pudding). The Holy Man will sing over the child to bless him or her with a long healthy life on earth. The Holy Man then feeds the sacred foods to the baby by taking a small morsel on his finger, which he places on the infant's tongue. This is to ensure that the spirits of the child embrace his or her ancestors' sustenance and recognize their relatives' abundant source of physical wealth here on earth. The Holy Man will then paint with *Wase'* (sacred paint) the face of the child with special symbols belonging to their *Tiyospaye* to mark the spirits of the baby as a sign of Lakota identity. The child is then given a namesake or Lakota name to imbue his or her spirits with longevity and a healthy life, as well as to protect and guide them through the four stages of life, from childhood to old age.

If the child is a boy, he will receive a rattle, one eagle feather and a small hunting bow and arrows painted with special designs for his protection. If a girl, she will receive a small doll and a dried painted cornhusk tied with a plume. Both boys and girls receive porcupine-quilled amulets. These quilled or beaded amulets are made in pairs. Amulets are important because the umbilical cord will be placed into one of the amulets; the other amulet is empty with only cattail fluff as stuffing, and used specifically as a decoy. The boy receives a *t'elanuns'e* (lizard) to ensure quickness in battle and the ability to rejuvenate quickly and heal if injured in battle. The girl receives a turtle amulet to ensure a long, healthy life, as turtles can live up to one-hundred-and-fifty-years. Once the umbilical cord dries and falls off the baby's belly, it is placed into one of the amulets and wrapped in sage. The amulet with the umbilical cord is put away from the public into a sacred bundle for protection. The decoy umbilical cord amulet is then placed with the child to attract and confuse evil spirits. If born as twins, both babies receive snake amulets.

After the child is blessed and prayed over by the Holy Man, the parents of the child will then host a *Wopila* (Thanks Giving Feast) to feed their invited guests and the Holy Man and to hand out gifts to those who helped with the blessings ceremony. Those presents can range from a simple thank you speech, a song, maybe a braid of sweet grass, to a more elaborate gift giving occasion filled with star quilts, sacred pipes, eagle feathers, etc. The ceremony can last a few hours to four full days to honor relatives and guests. The gifts and feast of a *Wopila* are based on a person's finances and wealth.

At each of the four stages throughout a Lakota individual's life, they are given a Lakota name to reinforce their identity as a Lakota person. At each naming ceremony a feather is given to the individual along with many gifts to ensure that the spirits of the person are strengthened and a solid foundation and roots in Lakota society are firmly planted. An eagle plume is tied to a conch shell from the ocean floor and between the two is fastened a *Hocoka* (centering symbol) or quilled medicine wheel. This unites the stars above with the deepest depths of the earth so as to bind the ties of heaven and earth together in order that the individual's life is straight and centered with health, vision and wisdom. Each ceremony, although unique in structure, is conducted with the same vigor as the first. *Wase'* (sacred paint) is anointed on the face and head of the person with special designs and symbols. A person cannot receive the feather and have the painting done without the songs that go along with these ritual acts of blessing. In this way the individual has earned the right to wear the face paint and feather, and is expected by the community to decorate themselves in public during certain ceremonies and feasts as a sign of prestige, and as integral to the identity of the Lakota Nation. This is a sign of the blessings of the Sacred Pipe and *Tunkasila* (the One Grandfather).

The main reason we have naming ceremonies is to instill our cherished identity as Lakota people into our hearts and minds with songs, prayers, and guidance. And we are passing down thousands of years of wisdom on to the next generations. Our naming ceremonies are elaborate and can last up to two or four days of speeches, sweat lodge ceremonies, feasts and giveaways. These naming ceremonies are not rushed due to the numerous laws and protocols that must be passed down to the youth. The child who is honored must know comprehensively and concisely what is being taught and shared with him or her. The paint must be applied in such a manner that is appropriate to his or her specific band. Each design applied on the body is sacred and has a rich and deep meaning; such as the way many Indigenous tribes around the world apply their skin tattoos. There is a specific meaning to the tying of the eagle feathers and plumes that must be told to the families. There are detailed and specific songs sung in special sequence that must be told to the children. The food is placed in a specific order on the altar, which is also set up in a detailed direction. This ceremony takes time to complete properly. A giveaway and feast is held at the end and the families who honored their children give speeches. Then the conductor will address the community and family. Finally the parents of the child will share their views with their children.

When it's time for us to make our journey back to the spirit world, we are anointed with sacred paint and symbolically fed the traditional foods of our ancestors just as it was done when we were first welcomed into this world at birth. Our name is called four times and the Holy Man blesses the body with sage and sweet grass. In ancient times it was the War Society's duty to conduct and prepare the body for burial. Today the Holy Men are being called upon for help, as the war societies are no longer active, they say. For the journey newly quilled (or beaded) moccasins are placed on the body, which is wrapped in a buffalo robe or star quilt. Gifts are given to the spirit for accompaniment on the trip. It is said that it takes four full days and nights for the spirit to complete the journey to the Spirit World and meet our ancestors. On the morning of the fifth day, it is said that the spirit of our relative has made it home to *Wichoni*. During those four days the family is to stay home and not go outside or wander from their homes. The family of the dearly departed begins the process of mourning and grieving for one full year. After the year of mourning is completed, the family has a memorial dinner with gifts such as star quilts, feathers, everyday necessities, etc. to honor all those who attended the funeral.

If we have fulfilled our promises to our Grandfathers on this earth, we will go directly back to *Wakan Tanka* (The Great Mystery), and recount our great deeds on this earth. If we have not fulfilled our visions and dreams here on this earth, we will make our journey back down The Road of The Spirits toward the South Direction on the Milky Way and there we will meet an elderly woman named *Maya Owichapaha Win* (She Who Pushes Them Over The Bank). She is standing at the center of the Milky Way where the path forks toward the south. There the elderly woman sits waiting and directly behind her is a doorway that goes directly south. She will look this body over and if we do not have the *hakitxo* (the mark) or tattoo, she will then push our *Nagi* (spirit) over the Milky Way Path and our spirit will come back to earth again and again or as many times as needed before we become whole, in balance and in harmony as a Lakota on this earth. This means we must keep our promise to *Tunkasila* and learn our customs, mannerisms, culture, language, and ceremonies, and practice them or bring shame to our ancestors, thus continue the cycle of *Phiya Txunpi* rebirth) or reincarnation. That mark on the skin, and that Holy doorway should always be in our minds and reminders to do well and good on this earth by our actions, and to live every day to its fullest by being a good and helpful relative to our families.

As Lakota people our greatest assets are our language, cultural mannerisms, behaviorisms, and ceremonies, all of which cannot be learned entirely by reading books and listening to CDs, as is the case of many who try to emulate the Lakota Way of Life. Some of our greatest leaders like Sitting Bull, Crazy Horse, His Red Nation, and Red Cloud all fulfilled our ancient ceremonies at puberty. Our holy puberty rites are critical to our identities as Lakota/Dakota/Nakoda people. These Holy Rites are not options or obligations, but rather are mandatory and a responsibility as parents and adults, and members of the beautiful, illustrious and rich Lakota "Sioux" Nation. As stated above, we do not integrate any other religious organizations or dogmas into our Seven Holy Rites brought to us Lakota people by our beloved White Buffalo Calf Woman.

This essay is for all Lakota youth and their families.

Four Souls

Trace A. DeMeyer

In this century of 80 percent Urban Indians sometimes we look for teachers, sometimes they look for us.

What we are taught as Native people depends on our teachers. Books serve as teachers, too, such as John Fire Lame Deer's *Seeker of Visions*. From different teachers I learned our four souls are evolving, imprinted with code. Our souls exist to journey, to experience, to give thanks. We are here to witness, to laugh. We are here to walk in balance and in beauty. Our purpose here is to "create," not simply live. To that end, each of us is given interests, relatives and gifts unique to us.

In my early 20s, my interest in healing began when I lived in New York City, where I met a reflexologist who told me about Cayce, Rasputin and other mystics. I studied quantum physics in my 30s after I heard a lecture with Fred Alan Wolf, a physicist. This was in Seattle in the early 90s, and Wolf was talking about trips to South America to learn secrets of how shamans work. (*The Eagle's Quest: A Physicist's Search For Truth In The Heart Of The Shamanic World*, Simon & Schuster, NY: 1991) Books by Native writers, what I could find, I devoured. My interests grew as I grew. Every Native person I met or interviewed for work had some effect, due to the fact I wasn't raised on the *Tsalagi* reservation. My being adopted made me appreciate every drop of knowledge.

Early on I learned: know whose territory you are walking on. In the East, I'm afforded the opportunity to pray at first light and thank Great Spirit for a new day. I pray with my feet as I walk on Earth mother with reverence. I introduced myself to the trees, streams and ancestors when I moved to the foot of the Berkshires in 2004. Since I live in Pocumtuck Indian Territory, I thank their ancestral spirits and sing to them when I'm near reported burial areas.

Priest, shaman, medicine person (man or woman) are titles used in books like James Mooney's *History, Myths and Sacred Formulas of the Cherokee* and *The Southeastern Indians* by Charles Hudson. Hudson and Mooney were not Cherokee or from southeastern tribes but used priest, shaman and medicine man interchangeably in their works. These men interpreted our culture as mythology.

Hudson wrote, "In addition to priests, or men of knowledge, the Southeastern Indians had ritual specialists who were born with unusual abilities. Modern Southeastern Indians call contemporary ritual specialists 'conjurers' and 'medicine men.' For the Cherokee and probably other Southeastern Indians, the main strategy in a curing ceremony was to cure the

illness by invoking the spiritual enemies causing the illness…
Another strategy was to achieve ceremonial completeness, so
the Cherokee priest usually called spiritual helpers from all
the four directions, and he repeated certain ceremonies and
formulas four times…"

Mooney wrote in *Sacred Formulas of the Cherokee*:

"Cherokee formulas furnish a complete refutation of the
assertion so frequently made by prejudiced writers that the
Indian had no religion excepting what they are pleased to call
the meaningless mummeries of the medicine man. This is the
very reverse of the truth. The Indian is essentially religious and
contemplative; and it might almost be said that every act of
his life is regulated and determined by his religious belief. It
matters not that some may call this superstition. The difference
is only relative. The religion of today has developed from the
cruder superstitions of yesterday, and Christianity itself is but
an outgrowth and enlargement of the beliefs and ceremonies,
which have been preserved by the Indian in their more
ancient form. When we are willing to admit that the Indian
has a religion …we can then admire the consistency of the
theory, the particularity of the ceremonial and the beauty of the
expression…"

A belief in four souls differs greatly from Christianity's one
eternal soul. The ancient Cherokee, and those who walk a

traditional path today, had a concept of the four souls that tie together beliefs relating to our physiology (bodily processes), doctoring, conjuring, witchcraft, death and funerals. Four is an esoteric number, as in the four cardinal directions: east, north, west and south and the four colors: black, white, blue, and yellow.

Many Cherokee believed in witchcraft and felt a witch could cause evil to happen by merely thinking it, and sometimes used conjuring for evil to extend his or her life. Witches could transform into other shapes, referred to as "raven-mocker" and "night walker." Priests or medicine people worked to keep witches from stealing the soul of an ill person. Fire and lightning, the principle means of achieving purity, were especially powerful against witches, according to Hudson.

Hudson wrote, "When Indians fell ill, Southeastern Indians turned to their belief system for an explanation and course of action. The organizing principles in this belief system were purity, balance, analogy and opposition, all of which seem metaphysical or magical to us…"

An *adawehi* was a human or spiritual being with great power. Only the very greatest priests were regarded as being *adawehi*. Hudson wrote, "In addition to illnesses caused by animal spirits, there were also various rules and avoidances. When he went to see a patient, the Cherokee priest would first try to determine the cause of the disease. If the patient has violated some rule or avoidance, the cause of his disease was easy to establish. But if this was not the case, the priest asked his patient to tell him about his dreams. Dreams were thought to be warnings of things to come." An example of a rule was when a hunter killed an animal; he'd sacrificed a part of the flesh to the "chief" of the particular species, an offering to show respect.

In Cherokee, the souls are each referred to as *Askina* (pronounced Ah-skee-nah; meaning soul, spirit or ghost). The following are edited descriptions of four souls come from *The Way of the Cherokee* by *Tsquayi*. White Chief Al "*Tsquayi*" Herrin was the leader of the Seven Clans of the Cherokee Nation of Sequoyah and his teachings were devoted to Cherokee history. (Their website: www.cherokeediscovery.com).

The first soul is the soul of conscious life, which animates the other three souls. This soul is human, not physical, is conscious, has memory, personality, immortality, and is whole in its essence. This soul is located under the top of the head and is found in saliva and other bodily liquids.

The second soul is the soul of physiological life. This soul is possessed by all animals, is a substance, has no individuality and is quantitative; there being more or less of it in the person or animal. This soul is located in the liver.

The third soul is the soul of circulation and creates blood.

This soul is possessed by all animals, is a substance, has no individuality and is quantitative; there being more or less of it in the person or animal. This soul is located in the heart.

The fourth soul is the soul of energy and is located in the bones. All animals, birds and fish that have bones possess this soul. The bone soul does not create physical substances but creates Spiritual energy, which can be used by the medicine person/conjuror to promote healing, treat illnesses that reduce energy, and as an aphrodisiac.

To live in a sacred manner, we are taught to smudge with sage and cedar and pray with tobacco (*asemaa* in *Ojibwe*). I take elders *asemaa* as a gift. Choctaw elder Mary Barnett shared how tobacco was used for many cures in the Five Civilized Tribes. The Cherokee made a concoction of tobacco juice one drank. Tobacco is/was one of the most important herbs used by Southeastern Tribes, she told me. My own grandmother Lona and her mother used tobacco. They chewed it, spit it and smoked it. Tobacco infused with good thought, a ritual act of "remaking" the herb, was good medicine.

Elders who became my teachers cured me of illnesses. In Lakota territory, Sarah, an *Oglala* elder cured me of a migraine headache in 1993. I inhaled a chunk of burning root deeply several times. Ellowyn (*Oglala*) taught me their medicine people could communicate with supreme beings our eyes cannot see. Invisible Gods, sixteen different beings, appear to their medicine people. I was taught we come from the stars and our souls travel back to the Milky Way when we die.

Healers, both men and women, will know people are ill by their vibration. Sacred sound, a drum or rattle or words, can shift our vibration. Our body is a container of four souls. Seeing in our container, those who can heal us see how we see ourselves. They can shift our perception, and uncover the roots of dis-ease. Not every disease is physical as people experience spiritual sicknesses, too.

Ellowyn shared how their Circle Teachings use plant medicines, certain foods and herbs, and a sick person is involved in healing their own condition. The Circle of Life concept: In the spiral toward perfection, each must accept to follow the medicine path, do vision quests, self-searching and use our intuition of the spirit world. The circle medicine triangle is physical, mental and spiritual. Responsibility for the illness or condition (and our self) is never taken away from the person. Using a sweat for purification, a cold plunge in water, dancing in a circular formation, represents our lives in a healing cycle. She shared a Lakota holy song:

O you people, be you healed, life anew I bring unto you.

O you people, be you healed, life anew I bring unto you.

Through the Great Spirit over all do I this, Life anew unto you.

It was Black Elk who said, "It is not I who cured. It was the power from the Outerworld, and the visions and ceremonies had only made me a hole through which the power could come to the two-leggeds. If I thought I was doing it myself, the hole would close up and no power would come through."

In the early 90s, I studied with Little Coyote in Seattle and learned about his Northern Cheyenne spirituality. He told me a story about a woman who fell in her bathroom and one soul was knocked out of her. Her husband noticed his wife had changed her behaviors since her fall and called medicine men to their house to retrieve her soul and put it back in her body. (And it worked.)

He said dis-ease (illness, discomfort) could have natural and supernatural causes. Curing by their men and women healers involved herbal and root remedies, purification, sweat lodge, smoking, prayer and sometimes surgery. Treatment would restore the patient not only biologically but also spiritually. At birth, *Ma'heo'o* (Great Spirit) provided the child with the "gift of breath/power" (*monotone*) and "spiritual potential" (*mahta'sooma*). These two gifts are developed through life.

Northern Cheyenne teach genetics as: The Material body is reckoned as female, deriving of one's mother. The Soul is reckoned as male, deriving of one's father. Four soul forces normally inhabit the Natural body: *Xamea mavo xooz*. The

Soul forces: *Hema tasooma.* Two of these soul forces are mostly helpful to health and proper conduct. Two of these soul forces are mostly damaging to health and proper conduct, harmful. Both pairs are antagonistic to each other and sometimes struggle physically within the body. Each Soul-force is capable of leaving the body independently, especially during sleep, but the Soul-forces might also leave two or three at a time. At death, the soul forces join together in a whole. Abrupt changes for the better (with healing) indicate that a benevolent soul force has returned.

For the Cheyenne, the purpose of painting the patient's limbs is to restore balance in the body, resulting in healing disease. The directional forces are in fact associated with the limbs, the person to be painted faces (east, south, west or north) when his (east—right arm, south—right leg, west—left arm, north—left leg) is painted with symbols for the cardinal directions. A prayer is said:

Salute the new moon with the left palm upraised.

Salute the new moon with the left palm upraised.

(Source: www.American-Tribes.com)

Little Coyote suggested I go to the Running Sundance in Rosebud. There is a protocol of respect when it comes to ceremonies. I called the Running family and asked permission to attend and took gifts, money, offerings, food and tobacco.

"Go quietly and gratefully when you participate in the sacred, like the Sundance and the *Inipi* (sweat lodge)," he said. With humility I went to the Sundance and purified for four days in mixed sweats. I made hundreds of red prayer ties. Little Coyote taught me you do not pray for yourself in sweats so I didn't, yet a painful rash I'd had since childhood was cured in Rosebud.

I learned to listen, be still, silent. It took many years. It took great effort to quiet the mind and silence the ego that had me believing I am important or unique. No one alive is more important than a mountain or stream or a plant or another human being. Only a fool believes their ego and acts.

How an elder accepts you will be based on respect you show them. If an elder feels you are ready to understand, they will share a story. When I met Pipe Carrier Dave Chief, an *Oglala* elder, he told me to watch animals where I live. They will protect us. If they leave suddenly, follow them. He told me it took him seventeen years to be able to serve as pipe carrier and helper to Chief Arvol Looking Horse, who is Keeper of the Lakota Nation's Sacred White Buffalo Calf Pipe. (Humility is necessary to be in the presence of the sacred.)

On two occasions I interviewed Chief Looking Horse and in 2004 he stayed at my house in Connecticut on a visit to the Pequot Tribe. I was humbled to speak to this sacred man, to be in the same room with him. Dave Chief told me Chief Looking

Horse keeps the most sacred pipe that connects our prayers directly to the *Wakan Tanka*, *Tunkashila*, Great Mystery. Smoking the pipe is a solemn occasion and is only done after prayer and ceremony. (I know prayers must be focused, unselfish, about gratitude and not about me.)

The Cheyenne say, "The pipe never fails." Nothing sacred begins without first offering the pipe to the Sacred Persons who dwell at the four directions, to *Ma'heo'o* (Great Spirit) and to Grandmother Earth. When smoking the pipe, only the truth is spoken and nothing but the truth. Smoking the pipe and being a pipe carrier signifies a person is of good heart and being truthful.

Whenever I've interviewed great leaders in Indian Country, they display generosity, strength, courage and wisdom. One of them was Cherokee Chief Wilma Mankiller, a wonderful storyteller who has since passed. I'm aware many of our leaders are born with clarity of vision and strength. They listen. They lead their people by knowing differences in opinions and finding the best outcome: that way their respect is earned.

Another great leader is John Trudell. I've heard him speak on more than one occasion and interviewed him at the Mashantucket Pequot Museum in May 2000. Trudell speaks in layers of meaning, with a quantum effect: it's understood by heart and mind. I'd hear him then study the transcript and find deeper meanings. I asked him about his ninth album Blue Indians and the unusual name. "I called the album 'Blue Indians' because there is a kind of spiritual and cultural genocide perpetrated on everyone that is poor in this country," he told me. "The advance of technology has put all of us on a kind of reservation. These are the people who can't educate their children or afford health care. They've been robbed of life which is what happened to Native people, so in that context, we're all Indians. We're not taught about our personal relationship to power. We're not taught about our relationship to the Great Spirit. Recognizing power is what you have to do. When you recognize it, you exercise it. You can't take back what they have already taken but you can stop the taking of your power, once you recognize it."

I learned our "feelings" could energize our mind-body. We look at our feelings when body functions go awry. As we think, so we are. Water can hold emotions and thoughts, which science just discovered but Indigenous people already knew. Our feelings can cause allergies, chronic-fatigue, depression, fibromyalgia, hypertension, migraine headaches, phantom pain, post-traumatic stress disorder and arthritis. "Knowing Thyself" is a core principle in many healing teachings.

Joseph Enos, a Pima Medicine Man, said, "We consider ourselves, our bodies, very sacred. You would want to go with what the Creator gave you."

Residue of past hurt, trauma and oppression poisons many today. Generations carry the residue that will continue until we release it. I was taught people must let go of pain (ancestral and present) and forgive past atrocities done to Indian people. After this, we are able to love others and ourselves.

There is great humility in knowing that you do not use your eyes to determine who is a Native person today. Indians are a diverse people, especially in the East. The Pequot elders taught me this. Stories of survival differ from western tribes since contact here in the East began with conquest over 500 years ago. One Pequot woman leader told me, "We've been cleaning people's houses over the past 300 years." Native blood is mixed with different tribes and other nations' blood. They do not look like our western brothers and sisters. There are many Indian people living east of the Mississippi, though many are not recognized. History has not shared their survival stories.

From my teachers, I am reminded I must be willing to give everything I have. I am an elder now and have more to give young ones who need me. The circle I make will touch many, many other circles. I give more than I take. I nurture my four souls. I pray my thoughts are good for who I truly am. I will pray for future generations as my ancestors prayed for me.

In 1994, Sarah, Ellowyn and I were driving to a memorial

and counted nine hawks. "A very good sign," the Lakota elder told me. "The more hawks you see in a day, the better," Sarah said happily. I have counted hawks ever since.

American Indian Healers, Staying Medicine, and Tribal Laws

Clifford E. Trafzer

Eleonore Sioui sat in her home at Wendake, Quebec, the center of Canadian Wendat-Huron people. She sipped a cup of hot tea and spoke deliberately about natural law among Wyandot people. She explained, "It's not the plants, it's the spiritual power that heals." Plants are used in medicine ways, she explained, but medicine people must infuse them with the spirit to bring the healing power into them. Through them, a person may receive healing. That is the lesson she offered and one often repeated by medicine people, past and present. They say the healing power is not the person. It exists independently of Sioui and other medicine people. They know the existence of healing power and how to use it in both positive and negative ways. They also know that Holy People have charged healers with the power and obligation to heal those in need and bring people back into balance.

Medicine people use spiritual power, the highest form of Native American healing. They pray to bring the spirit power forward to infuse the plant with power and medicine intended to help the patient. This law is not new among tribal peoples, but an ancient concept that emerged at the time of creation and has been applied ever since. Healing power is part of creation and known to First Nations people through song and story that are not "fish tales that grow with the telling," as a reviewer for the University of Oklahoma Press once stated, but a reality among Native Americans. Contemporary people still call on the healing power to enter the patient and help them in their struggle for wellness.

Anyone may ask medicine people for healing power, provided it is done with a sincere belief in the power and in accordance with tribal protocols. But special medicine people with a direct connection with healing power are able to bring greater concentration of power to patients than common people and members of the community. However, American Indian healers, doctors, and medicine people are quick to state that they are not the source of healing power. They capture the power and direct it into the patient to bring about healing. Wyandot Eleonore Sioui, Quenchan Joe Homer, Cherokee Jim Henson, and Comanche Kenneth Coosewoon all said that creative power asked them to help others by healing people. In fact, creative forces demanded these medicine people to heal others. Often through dreams, visions, and direct communications, creative or supernatural powers selected and empowered certain people to do medicine work, charging them to help others. This still happens today, although healers are reluctant to speak too loudly about their commissions since most medicine people are self-effacing. Cherokee medicine man Watt Cheaters simply said, "I just help people." This is a common refrain because true medicine people do not brag or boast of their power, except perhaps in competition with other medicine people. They never advertise on the internet, sell hats or t-shirts, or advertise set fees to conduct ceremonies. Indian doctors are not "trained" like Western physicians. Instead, creative powers gave them a gift of healing, which elder medicine people or family members help them develop.

The same creative powers commissioned specific individuals to call on the healing power and deliver it to patients or people in need of healing. However, the methods used by different tribes and healers vary greatly. Healers sometimes use elaborate ceremony and sometimes the simple act of praying, blowing, touching, and talking to heal those in need. Some tribes enjoy deeply involved and ritualistic healing ceremonies, including Diné or Navajo medicine people. Others, like Cherokee healer Jim Henson use their own unique method prescribed by elder teachers. Henson explained that he learned his medicine way from his grandfather. When Jim was a boy, he lived and worked with his grandfather, but as a young man, he became "wild." He settled down somewhat but had not found his life way when he had a paranormal experience. One evening, the ghost of his grandfather visited him, in Cherokee saying, "It's time." At first Jim did not understand his grandfather's words. But when his grandfather reappeared and said again, "It's time," Jim responded in Cherokee, asking what his grandfather meant. The elder apparition stated, "You think about it," and disappeared. In time the ghost returned to ask his grandson if he had thought about his words. Jim stated that he thought his grandfather was trying to tell him it was time to act correctly and responsibly as a Cherokee man and leader. His grandfather then said, "It is also time to do my medicine."

Henson's grandfather had been a medicine man for years, and Jim had grown up helping his grandfather who used the items in a powerful medicine bundle to help his healing way. Jim's grandfather told his grandson to use his childhood experiences to guide his doctoring. Jim explained that he did not have the bundle; it had disappeared when the elder had died. To this his grandfather responded, saying that he had buried the bundle at the old home place and to go to a certain tree, take a designated number of paces from the tree, and dig for the bundle. When Jim said he would get a shovel and do that first thing in the morning, the ghost of his grandfather said, "No! You will go now." Jim followed his grandfather's directive. After some difficulty, Jim found his grandfather's medicine bundle wrapped in several layers of canvas and well preserved. When Jim kneeled down and unwrapped the medicine bundle, a forceful wind blew out of the bundle, infusing Jim with its power. He took the bundle home and not long afterward, people started asking for Jim's medicine. Thus he started doctoring Cherokee, following the procedures he had seen his grandfather conduct years before. Remarkably, people started getting well. The medicine worked. Since that time, Jim Henson has spent his life helping others by bringing the healing power to those in need, including troubled children.

In a similar manner, the Creator commissioned Comanche Kenneth Coosewoon to harness healing power and help others. For years Kenneth wrestled with his identity as an Indian man, a Comanche of warrior stock living in the mid to late twentieth century. He wanted to fit into society and had earned the respect and admiration of many through his prowess in all sports, particularly basketball and boxing. While attending Cameron College on a basketball scholarship, he began his lengthy battle with alcoholism that held him down like a devil. Kenneth lived with a death wish, acting in reckless, violent ways with mishaps and accidents that should have killed him. Try as he might, Kenneth could not kill himself. Today, Coosewoon says the Creator had other plans for him, but he had trouble finding direction. Kenneth stopped drinking for a spell, started drinking again, and then overcame his disease.

After seeking help through Alcoholics Anonymous, Kenneth devoted himself to helping others by directing an alcohol and drug program for American Indians in and around Lawton, Oklahoma. While on a retreat into the Cherokee Country with other directors of alcohol programs, Kenneth participated in his second sweat lodge ceremony. Wallace and Gracie Black Elk led the sweat lodge and began a lengthy friendship with Coosewoon and his wife, Rita. When all of the participants left the sweat lodge to eat, Kenneth remained at the lodge to tend the fire and ensure it did not spread into the woods. While he watched the fire, the flames popped loudly, sending several unique chips into the area that glowed blue. Kenneth heard a voice address him, telling him to pick up one of the blue glowing chips, which has become part of his medicine. He did so, and while holding the blue chip, a number of spiritual events occurred in rapid succession. A great wind swept through the camp. Thunder and lightning cracked above Kenneth while a light floated like a flashlight through the forest on the far side of the creek. A bird called to Kenneth, telling him to come down to the creek. When he walked to the edge of the water, Coosewoon saw the blue light diffuse and spread across the creek like a blue fog. The light traveled across the creek and surrounded Coosewoon while he still held onto the glowing blue chip. When Kenneth reached down to touch the light, he heard it say, "don't touch me." Apparently, the Creator had manifested as the blue light and surrounded Coosewoon.

The events frightened Kenneth but only to a small degree. But then the earth began to shake. An earthquake came over the area, centered on the site where Coosewoon tended the fire. As Coosewoon later explained, "the trees started dancing." At this point, Kenneth realized that something spiritual was taking place, but he was unsure of the meaning of all this paranormal activity. Soon he learned the meaning of these events. Immediately after the earthquake, Kenneth heard the voice again, saying "Kenneth, I want you to lead the sweat lodge." Kenneth responded, saying out loud, "I don't do that. I don't know how to lead the sweat lodge." The voice responded, saying, "get a dipper and a bucket," tools used during the sweat lodge ceremony. The voice told Kenneth, "I will teach you all you need to know. Things will come to you. And I will always be with you." The Creator told Coosewoon that He would always be with him to help him.

Kenneth Coosewoon, Jim Henson, and Eleanore Sioui are only three of hundreds of medicine people that work within contemporary Indian communities of Native America. They bring their healing power to people suffering from many diverse forms of illness caused by mental, physical, and spiritual ailments. Within the Native American communities of the Western Hemisphere, many forms of illness exist, including spiritual causes of sickness that result from transgressions of one or more people of particular tribes. The disease causation might manifest itself in many ways, causing an imbalance that affects people in various ways. Spiritual illness might create mental or physical sickness, largely based on the societal "laws" of specific tribes. All tribes have laws that tribal members must obey or face illness. Infringement of tribal laws may cause illnesses or death, and they significantly influence the health of Indian people, past and present. Those with power within Native American communities understand tribal laws and prescribed protocols.

Native American communities have numerous rules, codes or laws that affect the well-being, health and balance of tribal people. The health of people depend on the way they deal with plants, animals, places, and people close to their communities and those related by culture, language, song, ceremony, song, ritual, foods and other elements of specific tribal cultures. If citizens of the community break tribal laws, they put themselves (and sometimes their families or tribes) at risk for ill health, sickness, and death. These tribal laws live today and are part of every Native American community within the Native Universe of North and South America.

Thoughts and actions influence the health of others within the group, particularly a person or family. However, violation of tribal laws by people outside the specific Native community and culture may not necessarily influence the health of outsiders. The term, "Staying Medicine" best characterizes the internal form of disease causation. The term emerged from the scholarly work of Donald Bahr and his Native teachers. According to Juan Gregorio, a Tohono O'odham medicine man, "Staying Medicine" never "wanders." It always stays among the people, from whom it originates, but walking or traveling diseases, including diphtheria, cholera, influenza, smallpox, colds, measles, syphilis, and other communicable illnesses, move from group to group. Staying medicine originates among specific tribes.

Native Americans of California tribes have their own laws connected to health, including entering sacred spaces. In the early 1990s, the United States Forest Service planned to issue a permit to a foreign corporation to build a ski lodge on the slopes of *Akoyet* (Mount Shasta). Native Americans throughout northern California, southern Oregon, and western Nevada protested. All of them believed the mountain was alive and a powerful, living being. Many tribes believe that Mount Shasta is not an inanimate entity but a living, holy mountain tied to Native creation. For many Indian people any violation of the mountain, like the building of a ski lodge, could potentially create illness and death among Indian people of the region.

According to Pit River Indian scholar Babe Wilson, many Native Americans believe that at the time of origin, the Creator had placed a great basket inside the mountain that emitted goodness to the world. They considered the building of the ski lodge a desecration that could inhibit the basket's function and make people ill. The U.S. Forest Service dismissed cultural beliefs but ultimately dropped the project but not before the superintendent of the forest at Mount Shasta made light of Native American beliefs. He dismissed Native American cultural beliefs about power, wellness, and laws. He asked one of the commissioners if the Indian people really believed a great basket of goodness existed in the mountain. When the commissioner answered in the affirmative, the forest superintendent responded, "Well, if there is a basket up there that sends out goodness, it's not doing so well given all the killings, war, and hatred in the world today." The commissioner agreed. He replied, saying, "Well, just imagine a world without that basket. The world would be in total chaos." Cultural differences abound in the modern world. Too often non-Indians marginalize Native American cultural beliefs, concerns, and laws affecting health. They label such beliefs mere superstitions.

American Indian men and women enjoy many forms of medicinal traditions today based on the most ancient forms of healing known in the Americas. Since the beginning of time, creative forces placed power on the earth and universe that special healers access to heal others. Healing places, plants, animals and objects abound in Native America, but many people believe such cultural concepts have no validity or place in modern society. Still, traditional healing ways exist and Native American healers continue to use them to transform people and bring about good health. American Indian healers convert "spiritual power" into forms of energy they can direct into their patients to heal. Thus, they transform one kind of energy into another. Medicine men and women convert power and direct it to heal the sick and provide renewed health. The ways in which medicine people work the medicine varies from tribe to tribe, but it exists in the twenty-first century with the acknowledgement of many tribal people. Indigenous healers usually work the medicine for the benefit of others, using good medicine to do positive work and not negative harm to others.

American Indian laws and power affecting medicine still exist, and they continue to influence American Indian health. Codes live within each community or tribe. Spirit medicine still exists among tribal people, and Western health care providers working among Native Americans, especially doctors and nurses, would do well to listen and learn from tribal elders. Too often, medical and health personnel refuse to appreciate or understand tribal beliefs in spirit medicine, staying medicine, and Native cures, especially prayer.

In the spring of 2008, Cherokee healers Jim Henson and Beverly Patchell, as well as Comanche Kenneth Coosewoon, cured a woman of breast cancer. Separated by over one thousand miles, these healers harnessed healing power and directed it to a patient with stage four-breast cancer. Upon hearing of her plight, Henson stood up to pray, which he did for fifteen or twenty minutes in the Cherokee language. He then prayed in English asking the Creator for assistance and healing. Then he began to sing in Cherokee. At first, Henson's voice was quiet and low, barely audible, but with time he increased his volume. He sang an old Cherokee power song in his native language, a song he learned in Christian churches and a popular hymn known as "Amazing Grace." Henson prayed for the health of the cancer patient and told the friend to return home and smudge the patient, pray with her, and tell her others were sending the healing to her. He urged her to believe this.

A day later, at a meeting of the American Medical Association's committee on Health Care Disparities at the University of Oklahoma Medical and Health Center, Comanche healer

Coosewoon provided the opening invocation, singing for the benefit of participants. Coosewoon had earned himself a positive reputation as a Native healer, and after learning of the woman with breast cancer, Coosewoon prayed for the young woman living miles away. During his personal prayer, he stopped cold and summoned his power, saying, "I think we can get that cancer, yes, we can get it and get rid of it." He instructed her friend to meet with the patient, tell her of Coosewoon's prayer, and inform her that he would conduct a healing ceremony for her. "Tell her the healing power is coming, it's there already, and tell her to give thanks for the healing." In spite of the miles, the two medicine men in Oklahoma sent healing to the cancer patient, which ultimately destroyed the tumors and cleared her body of cancer.

When the friend returned, he told the patient about the healing sessions and smudged the patient in prayer. He also gave her some of Coosewoon's medicine, which she took eagerly and respectfully. After their last meeting and smudging, three weeks later, the woman explained that she had been to the hospital for a pre-operation consultation. Technicians had X-rayed her breasts to see if her cancer had spread. The X-rays showed she had no cancer at all, so her doctors ordered biopsies. An analysis of tissue indicted she had no cancer cells. Her doctors were giddy, delighted at her condition. She did not tell them that two Native American medicine men had conducted healing rituals and ceremonies. After four years, the woman remains cancer free. For Western doctors, the cancer miraculously disappeared, but when notified of the healing, Coosewoon laughed, and Patchell simply asked, "What did they expect?"

Indian medicine exists today in many forms. Laws governing proper actions by Native Americans also exist. Contemporary Indian people know the old causations of disease, illness and death. Many know the creation stories and songs connected to good health and medicine. Most use Western medicine today, but many still use traditional medicine ways, established in ancient times before the arrival of newcomers from Europe, Asia and Africa. This is the first medicine of North and South America, medicine ways that still have life and efficacy among most American Indian peoples in contemporary society.

Miracle of 12-12-12

William S. Yellow Robe, Jr.

I was once told that the opposite of being in a state of anger which leads to confusion and lack of clarity was to laugh. Laughter is an element which brings forth the essential element of life, breath. You are required to have breath in order to laugh. This element, laughter, is a basic human component to cure forms of oppression, suppression, and other forms of human misery associated with colonization. All Indigenous people can appreciate a healthy laugh. A good laugh brings your senses to a state of clarity and this is helpful in moments of being overwhelmed by elements that control your life, but you have no control over them.

In writing this story I was reading an article on-line regarding the death toll of the upcoming day of December 12, 2012. The horrors that would occur on this day were extraodinary and left a person feeling overwhelmed. Hell hath no fury like the Mayans-aye! I wasn't looking to attack any certain group, or individual. I have spent my time as a working playwright observing life. I have been able to some times get beyond the spoken word and contact the idea embraced by a character's line or a character themselves.

As in real life, sometimes, characters on stage can be forced to take outrageous actions because they are accompanied by a thought that could be completely illogical or irrational. This is the drive of the story, "Miracle 12-12-12."

Laughter is a better medicine and way of coping with the constant theft, appropriation, and stealing of the Native Tribal cultures, spiritualities, environments, relatives, and basic life sources. It isn't a question of pointing a finger of blame or guilt, but a question of finally coming to grips with the reality of a situation and taking the proper steps in preventing the unhealthy actions from continuing. Laughter takes away the fear from the mind and heart, and always the breath to restore the courage and strength back to the body. A wonderful gift from the Creator. I am thankful to be able to share this notion, this story, and I hope, a laugh.

Pinamaya.

So, uh, in honor of this 12-12-12 thingy, this is not to be confused with 1+2+1+2+1+2, I have something to share. You know how you are told not to talk about your friends, or family? Even if they are doing bad things.

Well, this woman, who used to be a friend, told me and I've never told anybody about this, even though she wanted me to at the time, I kinda' held it back but I thought today was one of those days where you should just let things like this go.

So, any ways, this woman, Vera, the Indian name she calls herself is "Lilac Spotted Wolf Smoking Camel," heard about all the talk of a new Native Saint. So she said she should be made into a saint since she was already a shaman.

I told her I don't think you can do that. She asked what I meant and I told her I don't think they have a workshop for that. Not in those "shaman" workshops they have at the Crystal and Sage Burners Book Store. So she asked me what she had to do. First mistake.

I told her I think you have to perform three miracles. She perked right up off her easy chair and said she had done three miracles. I asked what they were. She said she had taken her whole body and entered through her sacred medicine hoop and came back.

I didn't think that really was a miracle. How hard is it to slide through a hula hoop with glitter and ribbons on it? I remember that one too, because she gave me all this opened Spam because she had taken out all the gel to grease the hoop. She does it now, eats all the Spam, since she gave up chili cheese nachos night at the Town Pump Deli.

Her second miracle she performs, according to her, is that she has these "medicine" cards. These are supposedly super hybrid medicine cards. When you shuffle them with your fingers, they smell like tea tree oil, both the cards and your fingers. And they have images of these weird animals like a jack-a-lope, loch ness monster, fur trout, were-dachshund, and one important one, a "Bigfoot," or Sasquatch. But every time she pulls out the

Sasquatch card, the image hides. She says it is there when she pulls the card but when she looks at it all she can see are a few trees. I told her I don't think card tricks, or readings like that count either. I feel bad for her, oh well.

Her final miracle is that she knows all the words to the "Star Spangled Banner." She can sing it and crack all her finger and toe knuckles while she sings, sort of like impromptu hand-boning. She did it one time and got really dramatic and at the very end, she farted. I don't mean to embarrass her, but it is true. I told her I still don't think this one can be counted as a miracle. She told me I had finished my tea so I better leave. I did.

I guess even with this 12-12-12 thing she won't be a saint. I told her she should start small. Go to Pamida and become a greeter like they have at Wal-Mart. I told her to take her motor chair with the card table and she could practice her cards, but I guess I should have told her she should ask the manager of the store first, huh? Oh well.....aye!

Above the Fire

Bobby González

The Taino of the Caribbean islands were the first Indigenous peoples to be overwhelmed by the catastrophic series of events that began on October 12, 1492. Over time we were bereft of most of our language, our songs, dances and ceremonies. Also, the prominent role of the woman in our society was supplanted by a machismo mindset that is still in power today. The poem "After the Fire" pays homage to Taino and all other Native Nations struggling to reconnect to their natural spirituality. It is, too, a tribute to the Women, they who are the cultural caretakers of the First Peoples of the western hemisphere.

Solemn observance.

> The sun hangs low in the sky
> as they start out.
> The sun,
> the great eye of the Creator.
>
> They bear
> objects of veneration.
> Sacred stones

blessed feathers
hallowed blood.

Ceremonies
rooted in ancient times.
Ceremonies
sensitive
to the seasonal turnings of the Earth.

Secrets unveiled
in silence and in solitude.

The powers of the mountains
are invoked.
A young apprentice
is initiated
by the Giver of Life.

Esoteric knowledge
bestowed by the Ones Above.
The dark cave is illuminated
by the light of distant dreams.

A worthy woman
stands in the heart
of the dimly lit cavern.

With arms raised to the heavens,
she intones a chant so powerful
that the floor of the forest reverberates.
The open circle of four
converges on the flames
that consumes a mosaic of offerings.
These selected men pay homage
to the clear-eyed daughter
of the traveling moon.

The communal dance
fulfills a cycle of discovery.
Age-old tales are retold
in whispers.

And the life
of one more generation
is sustained
as the smoke
rising

from the mound of dying embers
purifies the walls
of the voiceless cavern.

And the stars stand guard
over the enchanted dawn
which awakens
over the cloud
that rises
above the fire.

Part Three

Prayers, Dreams, Visions, Songs, Dances, Birth and Death: Beckoning the Nucleus of The Great Mystery

In Indigenous beliefs one does not just speak the prayer, dream the dream, visualize the vision, sing the song, or dance the dance but concretely experiences a personal power with these. We have long known that prayers bring healing and guidance in all forms, dreams and visions bring clarity and revelations, songs bring connection with all energies, and dances bring rain and cleansing, just as scientists have determined that music makes plants grow, etc.

The Great Mystery represents all that is familiar and alien about the Universe—where energy begins and circles back to again and again. While in human form one can, by the various mentioned methods, touch inside this unfathomable Sacred Center. We recognize there is, always has been, and always will be a Sacred Center from which we evolve and return, travel back to again and again. Birth is a re-coming, death a returning—constituent parts of the awe-inspiring cycle we experience as continuation of existence.

Pull

Duane BigEagle

The older I get, the less important my personal history seems. My culture, my perspective and experience, the times I've lived in, the ideas I've held dear and those I've fought against—these have shaped who I am. In many ways I've come full circle; at first imitating traditional prayers, now my poems seem again to be prayers and meditations.

> I pull the shirt off over my head,
> pull the covers up,
> pull feathers from my fingers,
> circles of smoke from my eyes.
> I pull dawn from sleep and generosity
> from the last bell of my strength.
> I shake debt out of my shoe.
> I lean back and loosen
> the rope from around my neck,
> from around my feet
> splashing down shallow creek beds,
> from around the spirits
> flying back to their home in the sky.
> I unbutton the top button

of the storehouse of linen,

the hiding place of all night dancing,

the pathway of necessity and tenderness.

I open the back door of summer night,

sip turquoise light

from the leading edge of storm

and pull long black hair

in writhing strands from the wind.

I pull names from silence,

a strong heart from laughter

and dreams from the nubs on raw buckskin.

I pull Native Nations and the good Red Road

from the spirits of the People

dancing and singing around me.

I grab time from the hands of the clock,

bend it into a hoop

and give this moment back

to the pure, bare, original day.

"Pull" was first published in the literary magazine *Zyzzyva*, Vol. VIII, No. 3, 1992, ©Duane BigEagle, 1992. Printed here with permission of the author.

We Speak the White Man's Language

Carol Willette Bachofner

As an Abenaki woman, I am always interested in the thinking of women about language as it relates to our culture. It seems to me that this poem addresses both language and oppression of women, but not in an over-the-top fashion. It is my gentle reminder that Native women (and indeed all women) walk a stony path. We are especially vulnerable in areas of language. What I tried to do in this poem was to open up the possibilities, to expose the raw truth about how we keep on sustained by our woman-ness and our tribal strengths. Even if our actions are somewhat subversive. The poem touches on cultural and religious restraints, imposed but not necessarily accepted.

except when dreaming, except when our fingers
braid hair, weave blankets, knot bait bags,
when we are praying in Indian. Work brings words
from the belly, the soles of the feet.
Words walk the woods where our relatives
burned the way forward from camp to camp,
trading stories with people along the way.

We speak in our own tongues, syllables full

of consonants, echoing from the back

of the throat to the nose, to the wind.

Our words are a clearing, a place for fire.

Where did the language go when the black robes

threw holy water on it? Did it disappear

when the switch was on our backs? Into the trees,

into the streams, into our wombs to wait.

"We Speak the White Man's Language" appeared in the 2012 collection, *Native Moons, Native Days,* Vol 7 Native Authors Series, published by Bowman Books, a native imprint of Greenfield Review Press (Joseph Bruchac, ed.). © Carol Willette Bachofner, 2012. Printed here with permission of the author.

The Secret Fire

Lela Northcross Wakely

The following came from a dream: I was flying and saw a round-looking house with a type of thatch or reed roof. A man was standing in the doorway looking up, as if he were expecting me. I came down and he led me inside. There were pallets on the ground along the wall of the house; the fire and drum were in the middle so everyone could see the drum and dancers. I was led to a pallet and laid down. I watched the dancers and listened to the drum. I "fell asleep" in my dream—I dreamed a dream in my dream. This is what I dreamed, complete with poems. I would like to thank the editors for helping to fulfill a heart's request.

Hear now my children the story of Mystery's Fire.

Long time ago our people lived together as a great Nation of many tribes. There were many clans; many elders and all people knew fire across the great Turtle's back. Now, the fire I speak of is not the same, nature's fire is but the trickster's way of trying to confuse you. The fire I speak of is why we are named People of the Place of the Fire, Keepers of the Fire, People of Fire.

Long ago visions were given by the Great Mystery of what

was to be and how to prevail against the woes to come. But something happened; what, this speaker does not know. Pride? Hate? Bitterness and despair, perhaps. Something caused our people to reject the sacred fire and forget its original purpose. Forgotten even as a legend is the man with hair the color of sunset flame. Braided into that hair was the eagle wing. Every feather known and unknown to man was worked upon his garments so that each of his movements was as a mighty flock of birds, and the sound of that movement was ever changing. Now the sweet blue bird's song, now the high call of geese, and a story could be heard for each feather.

He was of the Firstborn. His bold journey to the Blessed Land of Creation, how he asked and received assistance is not recounted in this tale. Although, without his quest, this tale would not exist. His weapon was a single bow and arrow, though no one ever saw him use it. Made from the tree that has no name in this world, its like has not been seen before or since. The Bow was made from a single branch of That First Tree and strung with a hair from the Firebird. Many choices were made at that time, oaths spoken. The Bow had only this to say at the time of her choosing. Until our people are renewed, she will not speak again. Hear now the words of the Bow:

I Say This
Freely do I give to you
Freely receive
Without burden of thanks
Freely give to others the same
As Fire gives warmth to all who draw near.
Go now,
Face the new fire
Fearlessly
Dance the new dance.
Find
And restore way
Of the Sacred Arrow.
Against that day
I have put my life
Facing the dawn-fire
And asking
How long?
How long?

The Arrow's head was worked from obsidian. The color was neither red, nor black, nor clear, yet were all these alone or together, depending on the eye that beheld the Arrow. Many songs of warriors' praise have been sung about this Arrow. Alive it was and alive it shall ever be. Alive and independent of the firebird. Its name was long and not for social use. You may call him Arrowheart. Yes, that is the closest you may come to his true name and purpose. Down by the clear waters, before that life-giving tree, his choice was made and affirmed by his words. Arrowheart's Affirmation:

I am obsidian
Held by Creator
As chips of my life
Fall away.
Revealed
Is a two-edged
Point
Of substance and time.
I pierce hearts
Dark with doubt
I cut asunder
Bonds of fear.
The hand of Creator
Fits me to the bow.
The touch is firm
The aim fixed.
Marked

Is the heart
Free
Is the soul
I touch
I pierce
I heal.

The woman with him was as golden as a sunrise shower that naturally refracts and shows the light for what it is—a blend of all colors and unconscious of just one hue. Her eyes were unique to behold: one blue eye to see beyond all things of the world and into the spiritual world, one green eye to behold the birth of all things in this world and in the spiritual world. Her dress was of soft hide from every animal known to us. Beaded in a curious design were the seeds that grow and nourish all things of this world. Do you see seeds you do not recognize? They are spiritual seeds, and who knows in what heart they have been planted, waiting to grow. Her leggings were woven of leaves but her feet were bare and brown like the earth she stood upon. She was of the Ones Before Creation. Her coming was like the soft spring wind that gently moves the leaves to grow. After she passed by, you could always smell a scent of rain upon fresh earth, and to everyone this scent brought a different memory. Memories of budding flowers, warm ripened fruits, the harvested husky smell of stored nuts and grain.

Now little children, do not misunderstand. Even though they were separate, they acted and spoke as one. Ah, yes, they were the two-headed Firebird. The two-spirited Firebird. Theirs is the healing fire, the life-giving fire that at once consumes and creates, brings an end and a beginning of life. Yes, the two-headed Firebird was not for all eyes to see in spirit form. It was enough for the people to see them walking the earth in earthly bodies.

They brought us knowledge of how to use fire to cleanse the land and renew the cycles of life. Many peoples no longer do this in remembrance and do they not suffer the effects of the uncontrolled fires of excess? Just as we ritually burn the land so she may grow and prosper, so we must burn away the old underbrush of our hearts. Leaving the ground purified for the rebirth of healthier ideals.

Of all the many uses they taught us of fire, the last and most important was the hidden fire—the Secret Fire. That fire which is held deep in all our people if they but knew it. "There will be ones," the Firebird said, "to come and kindle the great fires of the earth. All peoples, even ones you considered your enemy, must come to the Great House of Peace and allow the Secret Fire to grow. Look for them, the ones who know they possess the Secret Fire. After seasons of change without answers, ages without visions shall pass before they awake. They who are the Kindlers."

The Firebird said "they" because there will be many more than one. Only Creator knows the time and way of showing themselves. Who the Kindlers are and when they shall arise is hidden—even from this speaker's eye.

The Firebird instructed some of our people in secret ways of the fire. A new clan was named, a new society was created and given their own dance, private rituals and the Fire Medicine Bundle. A special blessing was placed upon them so that each generation would be born with the sacred gifts. Ah, but it was the adults' responsibility to teach their children how to use their gifts. THAT is where time and opposing forces have altered the ways, the teachings and meanings of those gifts until our people have forgotten they have them, or refuse to believe in the gifts. Or worse even, there are some who have listened to the voice of Evil One and say there never was such a gift, never was such a clan. Fortunately it is not for them to decide what Creator puts in each heart. Truly, I say fortunately, because this Secret Fire shall be the hope unlooked for.

The Firebird's last song was a promise to come. The Firebird said, "A new people shall arise to build a new nation. New songs will be taught to you. New ceremonies and a new dance will be shown to you. Look for them —they are coming: our children—the Kindlers. Learn this well and remember to teach my song to your children and to your children's children. Oh yes, even to those who are not your children. Teach to any and all who ask respectfully. Can you read hearts? Then do not deny a heart's request to fulfill itself. Who knows when the spark of understanding will start the fires within?"

Here are the last words of the Firebird spoken at the feast of partings. Many were at that feast, but few remember the departure of Firebird. A smudge was placed upon their hearts and minds so the pain of that parting would not be a burden to bear. But always the same words were heard, and great comfort it was to them. The Firebird said,

"Sing: By fires were they born
By fires within they were tried
And walked the path, unseen
Except by the fire's path.
Who shall see the little flames
Within the greater fire?
The Kindlers of the Secret Fire
In the fire's path.
Where shall it lead?
Who shall follow?
Flames hold the answers, unseen
Except by the fire's path."

So, the end of this story my children, is one of bright hope. Beyond all pain and loss, there is still this promise. Even you may be a Kindler. If you are, then your soul knows and bears witness to this story. And YOU know why we are called People of the Place of Fire. People of the Fire.

Give Thanks For Life

Georges Sioui

This poem came not from me, but from two clouds I was able to read and understand at that moment. I was fasting alone, I think in my third day. I remember seeing two clouds whose rapidly changing shapes inspired me deep gratitude for being able to see, hear and feel what their dance, their words, their song were saying. They spoke of the great love that we, humans, have to have and express every day for staying in balance and keep feeling fortunate and privileged to have and share life. I also understood very clearly then that life lived without gratitude has no meaning and leads to loneliness of soul and chaos.

> Give thanks for Life
> Every day
> To our Mother Earth
> And to our Father Sky,
> Then
> Speak,
> Sing,
> Dance:
> Speak the evil spirits away;
> Sing them to nothingness;

Dance to them as the spring-sun
Dances to the snow;
But to have words, songs and dances
True and kind,
Pray first, or
The evil spirits will lead you to ruin.

4 Those 2 Come

Keith Secola

The human race is the face of all people, different tongues, one heart.

4 those 2 come
Save them some

For the children living and the ones unborn
Give them shelter, keep them safe and warm
Hope and dreams and happiness
The world we leave them is a gift
Catch a ride upon a star
Find out who you really are
You think you're real shinny cool
You'll let you down to play the fool
Time to reinvent your self
Have to overcome yourself
Learn to live and love again
Find love lose yourself

4 those 2 come
Save them some

Stop and take a look around
Recognize what you're going through
Don't have nothing people just like you
Times are hard life is cruel
Angels sing, but angles mourn
Children grow then they're gone
Travel far and never far from home
A falling star on their own
For the children living and the ones unborn
Give them shelter, keep them safe from harm
Hope and dreams and happiness
The world we leave them is a gift

The song "4 Those 2 Come" is from the CD "Life is Grand." © Keith Secola. Lyrics printed here with permission of author.

Lel U Kunpi Kin Cante Mawaste (Because we are here, my heart is good)

Mary Black Bonnet

Tiwahe Wica Yu Wita Win

(Gathers Family Together Woman)

Tunkasila yapi, tawapaha ki han oihanke sni(he) nanjin ksto le.

Iyohlateya Oyate ki han wicicanin kta ca, lecamun welo

Tunkasilayapi tamakoce ki tewahila nan blihimic'iye

Tunkasilayap tawapha ki maka inhankeki hehanya nanji ksto.

The president's flag will stand (without end) forever.

Under it the people will grow, so I do this.

These are the words to "our" Lakota Flag song, which is played at Grand Entry for every *Wacipi* (Pow wow). It stands to unite the Lakota, *wasicu* (white), and "foreign people." The nations have never gotten along that well, so we are to gather ourselves under this flag in unity and make progress in harmony among each other. There is much misunderstanding, anger, fear and bad feelings among some in each group. But we are to live together under the flag.

This is what I was told from Albert White Hat, at Sinte Gleska in his Lakota Song and Dance class. For this class, we had to memorize a song and sing it, record it and turn it into him. I chose our flag song because it is so special to me. I locked myself in our small apartment kitchen and practiced, working endlessly until I had learned every word.

I am a *Wacipi* dancer as my *ina* (mother) and *at'e* (father) were before me. I was told by my elders that if we are able, we should dance for those who cannot. So I do. I dance for all that our people have endured, all that we will endure. I dance for the elders who may have been amazing dancers in their day, but can no longer dance. I dance for the sick, the elderly, the sad and broken hearted. Dancing IS medicine. I dance to honor my journey away from my people (when I was adopted by non-Natives) and my journey back to my people. I dance for our past generations and the ones coming up. I dance for my *ina* my *at'e*, my *uncis* (grandmas) and *la'las* (grandpas), my siblings, all my relatives. I dance for the honor it is to be Lakota. I dance for my daughter who is so beautiful and sacred.

So during Grand Entry, I'm usually in tears, not because I'm sad, but because I'm so overwhelmed and honored at this amazing culture into which I was born. As I dance, I am one small part of this giant, incredible, sacred circle. The drums pound away in my ears, hitting my heart, and I see and hear the dancers around me decked out in their finest regalia. These days, the best part is looking down and seeing *micunksi* (my daughter) dancing right along with me, in her regalia. Oh, how powerful that is, to be able to give her what was once stolen from me! She will never know a day that her heritage, her culture is not a part of her life. I am so blessed to live this life.

Hoksikiganan (Lullaby)

"I will tell some truths now. What we consider the most important thing on this earth is our children. The small baby boys and girls. What we call babies, we love, we cherish, and we want to raise them. Those children are those people who are living today. Once you were all children. They are put to sleep and are fed. They are looked after carefully. We want to raise them. So be it."

—Ben Black Bear Sr and R.D Theisz from the book, *Songs and Dances of the Lakota*

Micunksi, my daughter, oh, how she completes me! I waited so long for her precious little spirit to come to me. Every night, at bedtime, we have a routine that started when she was in my *tezi* (tummy). I read her the book "*On The Night You* Were Born" and then I sing to her the Lakota Lullaby. The words are:

Cante' was'te hoksicala
ake istima
Hanhepi ki waste.
Good hearted baby,
 go back to sleep.
The night is good.

And today, five years later, every night as she is crawling into bed, she asks me, "*Ina*, we are going to do my story and my song, right?" She speaks her Lakota language and is learning the Lakota traditions. She plays with other children and she loves "Sesame Street." Before I was a mother, I thought I'd raise my child culture centric. But now that I am a mother, I see I cannot do this. To do so would be selfish and hindering to her. Our tribal children need to participate in the greater world, learn its ways so they can use their knowledge, their skills to make the world a better place, to make life better for themselves and for their future generations. I do believe that no Lakota or tribal person can avoid walking in two worlds anymore. My husband once told me, "A culture that fails to evolve dies." And there is a difference between evolution and assimilation. Until I had a child, I worried to walk in two worlds was assimilation, and I did not want to raise an acculturated child.

We will not defeat acculturation with weapons and wars, but rather with the next generations armed with the active knowledge and practices of their culture. So alongside watching "Sesame Street" and playing computer games, I think we need to be teaching our children their tribal ways of life and their language. I am doing this with my daughter and I began by speaking to her in Lakota from the time she was in my *tezi* and speaking it to her for the first three years of her life. Our Lakota ways are always daily events, so she knows no other. *Inipis* (sweat lodges) and ceremonies are a way of life for her; her *la la* (grandpa) is a medicine man, so this way of life is as natural to her as breathing. She goes with me everywhere I go, so that she meets new people, sees how to respectfully greet and visit with her elders, and how to use the language and to hear it spoken by her elders. She is a ray of light and makes everyone around her happy. I have seen her interact with others who seem very grumpy and stand offish, and she will smile at them or say "Hi!" and they break into a smile, and their whole countenance changes.

Birthing my daughter was completing a circle in my life. I was taken away as a young child and raised far away from my culture; what I knew about the Lakota way of life I learned from what I felt in my heart and what I read in books. But now I am back home and determined to make sure my daughter will always know her culture, her ways of life.

Tunkasila (Great Spirit) has big plans for her, and I'm so grateful that I was blessed with the gift of being her *ina (mother)*. In Lakota way, we believe that we chose our parents, our lives. My husband and I wished for her as much as she wished for us. Every day with her is a blessing, another beautiful gift of how wondrous the world is. Being a part of my culture again, raising my daughter in our culture, all these things let me know I'm exactly where I'm supposed to be and doing exactly what I'm supposed to be doing.

Now as we hold hands and dance together to the Lakota Flag Song, in my regalia made by my *t'uwinla* (auntie) and her regalia, made by her *unci* (grandma), I see tradition growing, getting stronger and continuing for another generation. And passing the love and the tradition of dancing on to my daughter makes me happy. My heart feels good.

Tangled

Kim Shuck

My understanding of physics is imperfect, but I have had the pleasure of raising someone who can navigate those belief systems with great skill and am grateful for his tutoring. My understanding of a historical Cherokee worldview is imperfect, but I have had the joy of knowing relatives whose traditional storytelling was far more fluent than my own. I live in a city, on hill. A bus runs up that hill. I have a garden in which there are plants my gran would not have imagined, spiders she never met and a piped under creek which notion would probably have made her laugh (particularly now after recent rain when the creek returns pipe or no pipe). I am pleased to live in a time when people are studying the Higgs Boson and we are seeing a volume shift on the older stories. Each traditional person invents our world for the moment at hand, just like everyone always has. I don't know what my gran would have made of my cluttered house and my penchant for spiced tea. What I do know is that the more I learn about all of my family background and the more I learn about theoretical physics the less contradiction there seems to be between the views presented. Spider and the rivers (long men) and dawn songs are old news in Cherokee traditions. I think that my little secret with feathers is my own, but I may have borrowed her from elsewhere. According to the Max Planck Institute the Milky Way contains ethyl formate, the thing that makes raspberries taste the way that they do. Particles do move in synch in a phenomena called entanglement, something that I have heard physics folk refer to as 'a bit creepy'. Black holes sing in B flat. Our reality is infinitely delightful as it putters through its process. Oh and, raspberries are my favorite.

Dawn and I am singing to the east and the sky lit red, the sky with the fatter wavelength light. I am singing to the idea that everything is strange and potentially will behave strangely, be changed by my gaze, and is essentially the result of a complicated set of agreements between the tabletop and my palm and the plate. I am singing transformation to a world that is constantly transforming. I am singing connection to a wildly entangled world. I am singing my experience of time to world bits that could not care less about linear time, that can change and slip sideways through time to redo and overdo any moment that any bit of it chooses. I sing to the world rich with mystery with exploration. I sing to the trickster state of being.

Spider, mistress of fire, tangles particles into a web arresting their spin. Webbed particles are in a known place and Spider, heroic as she is, likes knowing where everything is. She is a creature whose understanding of the universe is both classical and modern at once.

146

She spins she entangles she tests her personal web theory over and over and her field notes are written in seed fluff, gnats, minute specs of dark matter and at least once, the sun.

How many particles of spin does a shawl dancer attract in the first dance after grand entry late on Friday with the smell of beauty and smoke and lard and strawberries and coffee floating into the arena from the food booth? As this one dancer spins, sings with feet and intention, other shawl dancers spin in sympathy. The deer woman looks on and does not move exactly with them. Physicists know how not to be taken in by deer women at dances. They can be identified by the velocity of their spin with respect to other dancers who are tangled in the drumming.

The child of transformation, the secret, pulls a cap more firmly onto her head to hide the soft feathers that grow just behind her ears. She sits by the beach where every second stone has a natural hole. She lets the water beat her heart for her. She has heard that things can be seen through such stones but she, small small mystery that she is, doesn't know how to control medicine, she only knows how to be a secret. She rests with her back against a rock without a hole. She sits and listens and sometimes snugs her hat more firmly on her head. The calls of shorebirds tug but the stones hold her down.

What would it be like to fall in the sky? What else would fall in some other place? Maybe she could slip through a turnip hole in what seemed like such a stable ground once. Possibly she could fall between the bits that make up the illusion of ground. Somewhere a grandmother is sewing with thread made of the pieces between all of the particles. Somewhere a grandmother is sewing a difficult quilt, a quilt made of unconsidered connections of forces without mass that are held together by particles of spin that push in the direction of good dancing, push in the direction of making.

Jay brushes his wings over a child's star quilt and leaves the reflection of his blue wings singing back from the surface. He and the Tobacco Moth watch this child of flying who has no wings for now as she sleeps in that charged sleep of small things. She is infinitely heavy, attracts more mass particles than the number of her atoms would suggest. Tobacco Moth and Jay give her the Blue of longing the blue of being pulled without logic of dancing with things that dance somewhere else for reasons that are not known. Jay wonders what this child with a flying spirit will do without wings but moth understands that with need, wings can sometimes be grown later.

The sunrise tastes of raspberries and somewhere sings an impossibly low B flat. I am a vibration until you look at me. I am a harmonic drawn from an odd angle in the stairwell or the strange gravity effected fold of space that longs so intensely that it learns to tug at things, learns to make unintended shapes. Even the light changes shape near some notes. Hands pressed tight against the wall of the bubble, I sing.

Long Man tells a different kind of time. Lit by this early citric light in a time of year when he is unfrozen, he tastes the poems of the woman standing on his bank. Some wishes have so many knots even the universe has to blink. Here and now, under a whisper rain, with this woman's prayers in his left hand, Long Man begins to laugh and the bubble membrane shivers and the gulls talk nonsense and every single thing rebalances and the unmaking starts all over again.

Dawn and I am singing to the east and the sky lit red, the sky with the fatter wavelength light. I am singing to the idea that everything is strange and potentially will behave strangely, be changed by my gaze, and is essentially the result of a complicated set of agreements between the tabletop and my palm and the plate. I am singing transformation to a world that is constantly transforming. I am singing connection to a wildly entangled world. I am singing my experience of time to world bits that could not care less about linear time, that can change and slip sideways through time to redo and overdo any moment that any bit of it chooses. I sing to the world rich with mystery with exploration. I sing to the trickster state of being.

Time Travel

Trevino L. Brings Plenty

Rethinking linear time, I confer with ancestral identity and ideological understanding that all time is now. If and when it is possible to extrapolate memory from bio-mass, what would that look like for the importance of existence? I start to think of how memory is reimaged every time we access it and how it makes me think about the concrete validity of the gain experienced. The construct of time and its implications on existence, the variables that could be had based on interpretation, the human body as a conduit of untapped information, to access it, and reconfigure it for our purpose is something I enjoy thinking about and opens many fantastical themes.

We draw in the absence of mind;
seek it as a chrononaut* suit.
The machinery of this body
imprisons us to its mechanics.

We forward our memory to the past,
the blueprint of our actions
triggered by outsourced impedance.
The simplicity of geometry

constructed of an architecture
of salient totem elements.

We attract like to comprehend
the sensation of loss as a potentiometer,
dial it to the purpose borne to us.
We peel the membrane,
lightning our images,
and we name it ancestors,
genetic map, comfort, and home.

* chrononaut—a time traveler.

The Year of Terrible Things

Wayman Harjo StandsStraight singing

Dawn Karima Pettigrew

"The First and the Last. The beginning of days and the end of days."
My great-grandmother, the midwives and the medicine women whose
legacy she learned whispered this into the ears of tribal newborns.
Once tiny warriors journeyed to earth, they ended their days among
the stars and began their lives in the line of time until time and space
returned them to Hesaketamese, Creator, The Ultimate Beginning
and Ending. My great-grandmother saw this particular birth that
defied death and transcended the time of life, when Creator, The
First and The Last, intervened, which we, as Creek people, always
expect that He will do.

Tal Vez sees light first. He presses past blood and water, vapor
and warmth into the portal between living and life. While
everybody in the StandsStraight and Harjo families turns 'bout
crazy, hollering around and monkey jumping out in the front
porch, I take my time. I am careful about things even now and
that must have been the start of it.

Tal Vez and I curve my mama's belly away from the lean line
of her slender frame. Marthel Harjo StandsStraight is only 14

years old at the time, which means scant room for Tal Vez and me. I find my place behind him and stay. He breathes for us both as the doctor's stethoscope circles chilly rings around my mother's back and belly. His heartbeat masks mine. When we finally come to the light, his shadow alternately embraces and engulfs me.

So my daddy, a teenaged preacher who married early to avoid throwing dice with temptation, fornication and malnutrition in no particular order, is shouting on account of Tal Vez being his firstborn son. I get to missing Tal Vez. I decide to join them.

I stretch my legs forward and get to marching, left right left. My legs and arms tear into tissues and bruising blood vessels. Finally, my right foot finds the kind of cold made out of air and fear. Every female relation I have gasps-all together, at the same time—like an unearthly, tribal choir.

"Scared every one of us 'bout to death," Great-Granny Bone likes to tell. She never minds telling about how I entered the earth on account of how it all turns out.

"Here we was cleaning up after your brother and out came your lil' foot. Nobody even knowed you was in there.

Well, I am and now I cannot get out. My other foot fails to find the first one, so I pull my right foot back in.

"Scared us right into acting," is how Great-Granny puts it. "Pouring Clorox and lighting candles. Your poor mama was just a-hollerin'. Pleading for Jesus, which ran right into the celebratin' out in front of the house and got lost underneath all the congratulatin' goin' on out there."

Meanwhile, I am preparing to swim. I can either tear my way from this tunnel of blood or drown in the rising water surrounding me. Either follow Tal Vez into the light or make this cavern of flesh into my casket. Disappear, then return as a ghost that fills gossip and inspires little children not to sleep without the lights. Only Tal Vez would ever know for sure that I had ever been.

I draw my legs into the rest of my body. My arms flail up and down as my lungs fill. Again and again, I thrust my legs before me as I lift one arm against all the water and force it from me. As I bring down one arm, the other rises. Water swirls around my head. I cartwheel.

Mama screams. My head and my arms find air. All that brightness makes me shriek, too.

This, my daddy hears. He abandons his gleeful romping with his in-laws and his cousin Jack to burst through the screen door and stomp into his bedroom.

"What in the Name of....?" Daddy starts to ask. As soon as he sets his eyes on my head and shoulders, he reaches out. Wayman StandStraight made me in God's will and now, he delivers me into it. Great-Granny cusses. Nana Standstraight throws a sheet over my Mama. Cousin Oklahoma StandsStraight falls out. Grandma Harjo asks for a favor from God.

Mama dies.

Daddy holds me in both of his big hands. Great-Granny takes up a spoon, holds it up to Mama's once-rosy mouth, now gone all slack and pale. She waits for a mist that does not come.

"Wayman, son, I'm so sorry," she weeps.

Later on, folks will try to make this a miracle and give all the credit to Daddy, on account of him being a preacher and all. And maybe they should because Mama really was dead and gone and now she's not. But to hear Great-Granny tell it, the miracle maker is I.

"Your daddy set you down on the bed beside your mama and laid his face down in the floor. None of us ladies could think of anythin' better to do so we got on down there too. Couldn't nobody pray. Too scared and sad all at the same time but we handed God our hearts and just laid there bawlin'."

Until I sing.

The Weight of A Grieving Heart

Death rubs long legs together,

A violin signaling famine,

Sawing the air with chitin and lard,

Promising lack in minor keys,

Preaching hunger while gnawing plenty.

A thick, black cloud, every insect for himself,

A wise man sees trouble and hides himself

In damp cellars of sorrow and pantries of grief.

The simple goes on and is destroyed

By loss and reservations in sharp succession

Until every man does what is right in his own eyes,

Which is almost, always, achingly wrong.

While the locusts laugh,

We fold our hands and eat our own flesh.

Enemies of death

Wait for singers who know redemption's song…

"You just started cryin'," recalled Great-Granny, "and next thing we all knew, your Mama was cryin' too. Water streamin' over her cheeks and over her hair and ears. And there you was, showin' off how you had lungs."

We never do know if Mama came back for Daddy or for me or for all of us, so we split the difference and give God the credit. Mama came back sad though, like she had been somewhere wondrous and I had interrupted her magnificent travels. But whenever Tal Vez's shadow blocks my portion of the sun or folks at church tremble when I look their way for too long, I remember. The Good Lord turned back Death because of me.

Then, I start to sing.

End of the Universe 12/21/12 for my Father

Stephanie A. Sellers

As the astronomers of our current era tell us, the rare and powerful planetary alignment of Saturn, Jupiter, Uranus, and Pluto that moved into place around the Earth Mother several years ago has created irreversible and dramatic changes among nations, individual lives, and within the earth herself. On the winter solstice of 2012, the 13th Bʾakʾtun of the Maya expired and another cycle of time began. When my Native father (Cherokee/ Shawnee) died suddenly that fateful morning, for me it was only fitting that a man who had done extraordinary things with his life would leave on such a powerful day. I believe he was needed in the Cosmic Spirit World to help turn the great wheel of change manifesting a world better aligned with the Divine Creatrix, with Changing Woman's and Sky Woman's original visions of wholeness. When people ask me how an illiterate, destitute Indian man accomplished what my father did, I just say, "Courage and lots of Magic." To me, he embodied the spirit of the mid-winter king: no matter how many times he fell into darkness, like the sun, he always returned. This observation is at the cultural core of who we are as Indigenous people: continuance, healing, and life..

worn wheel turning rusted water
he carried copper tubing, pressure
slowly corroding the bones of
his left shoulder, the vault of his heart bent
for sixty-six years. I remember his handkerchief
mopping sweat, his lunch made by
folding bread in the dark dawn, the
thermos of coffee, enough to last
to Baltimore, Harrisburg, Frederick
wiring factory buildings outside in
winter, fingers burnt red with frost,
colored scrap wire twisted on my
child's wrist. I waited for his return
every day, listening for his truck
engine upon the asphalt, my photo
hidden inside the worn wallet. before
dawn he carried water to piglets and hens,
.22 rifle against the bull's brow every January
a sacrifice enough to feed a family until next year
eyes straining in the faint pink of clouds
like childhood mornings on a dairy farm
metal tines piercing baled hay, the Indian
boy unable to read who spent every living hour
governed by the turning sun

each moment ticking toward this day
when the mid-winter solstice struck
stones tuned by ancient hands carved
by deer antler chisels, winter snow
blinding as invisible memories
in a distant land where ancient monoliths listen
for their cue to signal that the hour had come
like the valves of his heart, waiting
under a December horizon of stars
living every day on faith.

did he struggle for air
or lift up his aching head once
more that winter day of slanted light
death deep and vast as the butcher's
soothing voice as he turns the latch
not wanting adrenaline to ruin a lifetime
worth of gentleness, for fear to become
his last memory
in the barn of hay alone, the bull
long slain in his earthen stall, my father
extinguished, their lives blessed forever
by their blood flowing among the living
resting upon the great oak boards of the

barn floor sawed by men's hands and
passed through paper sand to smooth
what had never meant to be rough
his last day the shortest of the year.

his heart exploded between morning coffee
and ten footprints in the snow, he tied
his boots just the same that day,
draw up snugly, right over left, pull through,
tighten, make a bow, squared nails on cracked
wide hands, red bird hopping in gray branches
of the lilac. searching the bare patch he shoveled
for sunflower seed. bitter cold between breaths.
lungs prepared at conception for this moment
to fall empty. destiny encoded his vessels, angels
counted each breath. while the sacred devout
at Stonehenge, Upper Peninsula, Peru chanted,
danced all night at their end of the world
party, waiting for the earth to crack and destroy
but here in Pennsylvania is where the fates
came to call. where the last pebble fell
from the maker's hand and the mid-winter king
disappeared into the garnet red sun.

Thoughts Concerning the Importance of Time Before Passing to Spirit
(*For my son Devon)*

Natalie Thomas Kindrick

My thoughts are everywhere, blowing around like broom sage on a windy day. I worry about what we have left for the seventh generation. Is it enough? Did we do "it" right? I think of our lands and how people keep building closer and closer to the boundaries. One day I fear I will step out of my front door onto someone else's lawn. Are we taking care? I don't feel it this morning; like we need to do more, pare down, get rid of the junk and focus on what is important: family, traditions, our stories passed down from person to person by words spoken, not only by book or songs.

I know that my responsibility—as I was taught—is to make my corner of the world a better place. I look at my children and wonder if they are prepared for the future. Can they handle the important things in life? Most of us live in the here and now, not bothering to look beyond. When it is my time to pass to Spirit, no amount of wishing or praying will get me a "do-over."

What I speak of death has been passed down to me from my grandmothers. They say this is the way; this is how this works; no need to be afraid...

Death is merely leaving one life and crossing the river to another life.

In the early morning hours as I watch the sun come up, I can feel that yesterday is old and has passed. Today is new. There have been times however, where I am caught in between. The distance is so fine—like the space of a hair.

I know one day I will leave this life, moving on to my next. I will not be able to take those lessons learned with me but must start anew. I will be given water and cornmeal for my journey to the Spirit World. I know the Spirit Horse is coming for me. There will be two riders on horses and between them will be a horse devoid of rider—this will be my horse. They will come for me when is it my time, and they will stop at the river and water their horses, waiting for me.

My time to go? I do not know when it will be. I only know that I want to take the time I have been given to do all I am called to do to make my part of the universe a better place for the seven generations. To do this by reiterating the importance of family, traditions and story. To teach my children to respect our connection to this earth and all its inhabitants. This is my duty as an Indian parent.

Part Four

Stories Old and New, Told and Retold, Spinning and Spinning, Keeping the Universe Intact

Stories are culture, the way we live, breathe, and survive... for without story and storytelling, we'd be lost. Traditional and modern storytelling in Indian Country uniquely provides us a manual, a roadmap, a star map, a guide to living for everyone who needs it - and it's inclusive, for all humans. *Ea Nigada Qusdi Idadadvhn* means All Our Relations in Creation; we are all related. Stories connect us all.

Story is who we are, where we come from, and where we are going. We are story stones on which sacred carvings are added daily. To honor those who came before us with a passageway, and solidify a purpose for those who will arrive, it is our responsibility to share these stories—olden and modern day—whether they are didactic or entertaining. In this fast-paced world of instant messages, texts and sound bytes, stories are a way to reconnect to the mysticism of all things. Every story is a living being, waiting to be fed by its respectful sharing.

No Man Likes his All Neglected ... Little

Basil Johnston

"No man likes his all neglected, be it ever so little." Samuel Johnson long ago complained.

Now, people like to be judged by the great men and women their nations have begotten. They like to be judged as well by the great works of art and literature that they have created; they like to be judged by the great inventions that they have brought into being; they like to be seen as the founders and champions of institutions. And some like to glory in war, conquest and the building of empires.

Our people of Turtle Island are no different from others who lament that their "all," ever so humble, has been neglected.

Our people too, long to have their heritage remembered as it was once inscribed on the teaching rocks and wrought into wampum sash and stored in the memories of our elders. They want to be measured not by what they wore, what they lived in, how they got from place to place, or how their society was structured, but rather how they managed to accomplish what they did with but the most primitive of tools. But most of all they would like to be seen as partisans and champions of the liberties. They prized their right to come and go whenever and wherever they chose. Among them there were no masters, no underlings, all were co-equal. When they had a need to talk to the Mysteries of Mysteries, they did so in private in the forest or meadow or seashore, and what the Mystery of Mysteries imparted to them was theirs to understand according to the insight that they had been given. In their quest for sustenance and for the meaning of life they came to regard the land a mother that nourished, sheltered, clothed, healed, comforted, taught, and filled her children with visions of beauty. All her children had a place and a time upon her bosom, and all were entitled to share in their mother's bounty. What our ancestors saw taking place upon the land inspired them to ask, "What does it mean?" In their attempts to answer the question that they asked of themselves, our grandfathers and grandmothers gave their answer in story form, leaving us, their descendants, with a treasure-house of stories to enrich our minds, challenging us to add to their legacy. The language and the wealth of stories deal with themes, concepts, understandings, institutions, customs and morals, such matters that have drawn the scrutiny of all peoples from the beginning of time.

Missionaries who accompanied the interloping adventurers saw our ancestors as pagans whose beliefs were rooted in superstitions, and as backward peoples whose minds were incapable of taking in the abstract. For their part the chroniclers of the achievements of the leaders of pillaging expeditions recorded that the people they came across were backward who did not live in permanent settlements as did civilized people in Europe, but dwelt in makeshift camps made of bark. The savages' manners at table were of course compared to the refined, cultured manners of more advanced peoples. The writers reported that the people they encountered wore crude garments made from the hides of animals and that, having no sense of modesty, often went about half-naked. Their tools and implements were made of stone, wood and bark. They had a very rudimentary social structure; no government to speak of and no central authority. Poor were they. They had no churches, no schools, no cities, no shops, no art, no sculptures, no music, no castles, no armies. They came and went as they pleased, no sense of responsibility. For this our people were vilified.

Had the chroniclers looked further or cared to look deeper than what their eyes took in and what their minds could absorb, they might have deduced from our ancestors comings and goings the exercise of liberty that every man and woman was endowed with. They ought to have gathered that the natives had an intense sense of equality that they would not bend their knee before any man, or take orders.

Their kinship with the Mystery of Mysteries was personal, as were their beliefs. "Let me talk to the Creator in my own way, let me listen to and understand the Mystery's words in proportion to the talents that I have been given. You talk to the Creator in your own way."

Had the observer cared to look beyond the wigwams and the teepees, along with their drying meat racks, he might have seen that the residents owned their dwellings and the land the dwellings stood on, and that the produce they harvested was theirs to serve their needs; and when they shared their goods with the elderly, the sick and the disabled, they did so to fulfill a duty to their neighbors in seeing to it that their neighbors received their share of the bounty as a matter of right.

The land (*aki, aski*) gave our ancestors food, clothing, shelter, medicine, challenges, and knowledge, whatever they needed. Meeting and mastering the challenges gave our ancestors a sense of accomplishment and worth. With confidence gained from years of experience they could declare, "Yes! I can do that."

The land was their teacher, telling and showing them what they needed to know about life and living. Mother Earth (*Muzzu-kummik-quae*) nourished the body, soul, spirit, heart and mind. As teacher, the land was their book of knowledge; the insects, birds, animals and fish, their tutors. Our ancestors as learners had but to open their eyes and ears and all their senses to the teachings of the land, to take into their being what lessons Mother Earth had to impart.

She told them the most wonderful stories, not in words but in action. Through drama enacted by their co-tenants upon the land, Mother Earth showed the realities of life, deeds right and wrong, mischievous and comical. In the spring of the year she performed acts of creation; in the summers, the fulfillment of the promise of spring; in the autumns the coming to naught of the yield and beauty and the promise. In the winters most of life was suspended, and *Weendigo* (giant cannibal) walked the land while *Akeewaedin* (North) took hold of it in a snowy, deep grip. Though Mother Earth was covered with a blanket of show, she was but in a restful sleep, to re-awaken once more in the spring to re-create anew. With each awakening Mother Earth re-created life anew and inspirited the old. In the changes that took place, our ancestors saw transformation evolve in blossoms that turned into berries, vegetables and fruit; in the chrysalis that changed through two other stages into a butterfly. It was a wonder to behold. And our ancestors listened to the talk of birds, insects and animals as they listened to the voices of the thunderbirds. They watched as an invisible sculptor-artist created vistas of beauty in the sky with clouds. Even in all these changes our ancestors saw harmony.

From the phenomenon they saw and heard, touched and

tasted, smelled and sensed, our grandfathers and grandmothers made up stories for the understanding. Thousands of stories did they store in their memories leaving us, their descendants, with a good grasp of the natural world.

Long ago they observed the wariness of cubs and pups, offspring of animals who except for a few, went about tentatively. In this respect, humans and their offspring were akin to their co-tenants on the land. All were endowed with a measure of circumspection and self–doubt, which is not a bad thing, meant to serve as a means of protection. To dispel the fear and uncertainty instilled in their offspring, our ancestors invoked the *Auttissookaunuk* (the Muses) to come to their assistance in finding a way of infusing a sense of worth and confidence. Together with *Auttissookaunuk*, our ancestors conjured up stories such as the "Gift of the Stars" that carried the message every child is a precious gift to its parents and the community and that every child has been endowed by the Mystery of Mysteries with its own precious gift that will, when found and nurtured and shared with others, bring untold benefits to the bearer of the gift but also to many others as well.

Only selfishness, "Self," the "Me," the principal source of all human ill-will and malevolence will hold back men and women from sharing their talents with their neighbors and in doing so will breed resentment. For what good is a sweetness of voice if there is no listener to hear it or grace of form if there is no one to behold it. With such understandings these and others, our ancestors sought to instill selflessness in the hearts and minds of youth.

From the large number of stories that our ancestors conjured up concerning *Nana'b'oozoo's* (spirit being who represents a caricatured understanding of human nature who is not what he appears to be; his real character is hidden, and he himself does not see things as they really are) failure to carry out his good intentions owing to this giving in to the demands of his "Self" and its distractions, suggests our grandmothers and grandfathers had a good idea, understood the principle that strength of character is the dynamic that will fulfill talent. With resolution, patience, dedication, single-mindedness, hard work, talent may as well be buried.

It is good and fitting that our people mean to press the governments to include North American Indian teachings, beliefs, understandings, perspectives, customs, history, literature in the curriculum in schools and into our lives for the lessons conveyed in our stories, though ancient, still have application to life today.

We may not be able to point to a galaxy of great men and women as evidence of our merit, but our tradition did not exalt individuals above their co-equals; we cannot furnish great works of art or literature or inventions as do other races, but our people are no less loving of works of art; daily they look upon the great works of art and sculpture wrought by the greatest artist, the Mystery of Mysteries, in the skies, on the landscapes and seascapes; of symphonies composed and performed by birds, frogs and winds; of ambrosias welling out from blossoms, flowers, fruit, berries, sweetgrasses and evergreens.

If our people are to be judged, they would like to be judged by their passions for and their exercise of humanity's most basic and vital of institutions, the liberty to come and go as masters of their lives and works, the liberty to talk to the Mystery of Mysteries, and to understand the teachings of Mother Earth according to one's capacity of mind and spirit; the birthright to the bounty of the land and to a place whereon to set their dwellings.

They would like to be seen and remembered for their stories relating what they learned from the land about life and human nature. Our ancestors left a rich legacy of stories for painters, choreographers, sculptors, authors, historians and academics.

What our people once had in abundance was beyond price, far more valuable than the silks, spices and silver that the intruders who chanced upon this continent were seeking. When they saw our ancestors come and go as they pleased, without having to ask permission of a master; stand, eat and talk with their leaders without subservience; keep the fruits of their labours for their own needs and to share them with the needy; and to talk and give thanksgiving to the Mystery of Mysteries, and saw men and women in possession and in occupation of homesteads on land that they had chosen for themselves as their own and which their neighbors acknowledged as belonging to them, the intruders coveted what our ancestors possessed for they had nothing comparable in their traditions.

Before long the intruders put silks, spices and silver out of their mind. In the centuries that followed, the intruders dispossessed our people of their lands, institutions and rights and imposed upon them the master-servant relationship and all that implies.

It is good that our people know the richness of the heritage of our peoples. For the community to include our literature, geography, botany, zoology, educational methodology, harmony in the jurisdiction's education system would bring benefits to our youth, yours and ours.

To know that our people had a treasury of stories that touched upon a wide range of themes bearing upon life, human character and conduct, teaching and learning, custom and astronomy, botany and zoology, government, rights and duties that will confer on youth a sense of pride in their heritage and themselves.

To hear and to read the stories will provide youth other perspectives than those of Western Europe on such subjects as values and institutions that will enrich their minds and broaden their understandings.

To have a well-stocked store of literature will furnish our aspiring authors, poets, painters, sculptors, musicians, choreographers and filmmakers with a wealth of themes and topics for their creations.

The Creation Story

Barbara-Helen Hill

As a person of mixed ancestry, Haudenosaunee (called Iroquois by the French) and British Isles, I've been fortunate enough to hear many Creation stories or myths. I remember being surprised to learn the story of Adam and Eve is a myth or a form of the Creation story for one group of people while other people have stories that include the world coming from an egg. There are many books written about our Haudenosaunee Creation stories and many more versions than the one by J.N.B. Hewitt that I am now sharing with you.

In the Mohawk version of the Creation story, Hewitt begins with the story of the sky world and there being no death and no grieving. He then moves on to the woman in the sky world giving birth to a daughter who has no known father. The story then turns to a man becoming ill then dying. Before his death he instructs his mother to have a burial case made for him and says she would instinctively grieve, shedding tears. He tells his mother to use her best skills in creating the burial case, in dressing his body, and fixing his hair. He then tells her to place it up high facing the east. The daughter that was born with no known father grew rapidly and one day began to weep. They did everything they could to console her but nothing worked until they took her to the burial case and let her see the person inside. That calmed her for a while but when she began to weep again, they took her once more to the case where she was calmed.

They then built a ladder so she could climb up and see the burial case whenever she needed to. Often she was heard talking as if replying to questions or statements; other times she laughed. This went on for quite some time until she gained maturity and one day told her mother "her father" said it was time she was married. It was then they knew who her father was.

The father instructed the young girl to have her mother make corn bread mixed with berries and fill a burden basket with it. The young girl was to walk towards the east until she met a new group of people. She was to take her burden basket filled with the corn bread and she was to marry the chief of the group of people she was to meet, but he also told her that there would be trials and tests on her journey. (Hewitt wrote many pages of descriptions of the sky world and the trials and tribulations that the girl would face on her way to meet the man she was to marry.)

When she reached the village, she went directly to the chief who was lying on his bed and placed her burden basket of corn bread beside him saying, "We are to marry." He told her to sit on the other side of the fire. After darkness came and the people went to bed, he made his sleeping mat then made another sleeping mat for her at the foot of his. They did not lie together. They lay on their mats with the soles of their feet touching.

The story goes on for several pages about her work in his village, her tests, then him giving her venison he stored to fill the burden basket to take back to her village. In her village she instructs the people to share the venison and remove the thatch from their living places, during the night white corn hailed into their homes. They stored the venison and white corn and the young woman went back to her husband.

She told him all that went on in the village of her family. After a time he became ill and since no one in that village knew of illness or death, each of his advisors came and made suggestions as to how to help him. Nothing worked. They asked him what they could do to make him more comfortable. He told them if they uprooted the tree in his yard, he would lie beside it and might feel better.

It is said the wild cherry tree was adorned with white blossoms that gave light to the village. His wife was instructed to prepare a bed for him then to sit beside him. He then directed her to hang her legs down into the abyss that was created when they uprooted the tree.

He lay there for some time and then appeared to recover from his illness. He raised himself on his elbows and gazing into the hole where the tree had been, he instructed his wife to also look into the hole. When she did, he placed his hand on the nape of her neck and pushed her in. As she fell, he stood up and instructed his people to replace the tree, which they dutifully did.

The woman kept falling. She fell a long time through blackness and then she saw the dark blue. She didn't know what it was at first but then it became clear—it was nothing but water. Having seen the woman falling, the Loon instructed the water birds to fly up to her. Working together, they made a kind of platform with their wings and bodies and "caught" her as she fell. They then lowered her down upon the back of the Great Turtle. Because she couldn't last on just the Turtle's back, the Loon instructed the water animals to dive deep down to bring back the earth. They all tried—first the beaver and then the otter—and each time there was a longer period of silence before the animals floated to the top of the water—dead. Looking in their paws they saw no earth. Finally the muskrat said he'd try. He dove down and was gone a long time. When he eventually surfaced, he too was dead but in his paw and in his mouth was a bit of mud.

In the version I was told, "Skywoman" got up and began to

walk in the direction of the sun and as she did the earth began to grow, thus earth was born. In another version, the muskrats continued to dive and die while bringing up more mud to cover turtle's back.

In this version, when she landed on turtle's back and small bits of mud had been placed on turtle's back, she lay down and went to sleep. When she woke, the earth had increased in size and willows and shrubs were near the edge of the water. A deer had been placed beside a fire and a sharp stone to dress the deer. After she dressed the deer and had her fill, she noticed more herbs and plants and a rivulet; the earth had been growing larger.

It is said that when she started to fall after her husband pushed her, she grabbed at the roots and grasses and when she landed on the turtle she had in her hand the seeds and roots of the corn, beans, and squash with tobacco, strawberries and other plants. And when she fell she was also pregnant, eventually giving birth to a daughter.

There were just the two of them on the land, mother and daughter, with apparently no one else around. It is said that the young female grew rapidly. Her mother kept watch, telling the daughter that if anyone came to court her that she was to tell him or her she must ask first ask her mother's permission. They were not alone and suitors did come. One by one she was asked to marry and the mother when asked would say, "No, that is not the one." Then one day the daughter told her of a man with deep fringe hanging from the garments covering his arms and legs and the mother said, "Yes, he is the one."

When the daughter went to him and told him they should marry, he said he'd return when it was dark. He came to her, to court her if you will, but when she lay down and went to sleep he placed an arrow beside her—he didn't lay with her—in the morning the arrow was gone and he was nowhere around.

The mother soon became aware of her daughter's condition, how she was pregnant with twin boys. One day, she heard them talking inside of her. They were arguing about how to be born. When it was time for them to come into the world, one emerged in the normal human way of being born; the other one came out under his mother's armpit—thus killing her.

The grandmother cared for the two boys. She asked them which one had killed her daughter. The one who had killed her, Flint (because he was covered in flint) blamed his twin brother Sapling. Sapling, who was born with skin like modern day man, told the truth and said that it was his brother.

The grandmother believed Flint and cast the other child in the bushes. She took Flint and cared for him; it was amazing how much she loved him. Eventually she heard the bushes rustle and saw that the other twin had come back to her but again she told him to leave and never return. She made the moon out of her daughter's head and made her body into the sun. The grandmother loved the boy called Flint and did anything he asked. Sapling, the other twin, lived in the land nearby. He grew rapidly and made himself a bow and arrow. Flint instructed his grandmother to make him a bow and arrow as well. The two of them went about shooting their arrows.

One day the boy whose flesh was like that of today's man shot his arrow at water birds but they flew away and his arrow fell into the water. When he dove in to retrieve his arrow he found that there was no water there and he was beside a lodge. He looked in and saw a man who asked him to enter.

He told the young man that he was his parent and gave him a finer bow and arrow and two ears of corn. One ear of corn was still milky and he was told to roast it. The other was dry and he was told to save it for seed. After he returned home he kept running by the lake saying, "Let this earth keep on growing; I am called Maple Sprout." The earth continued to grow and the maple saplings formed themselves into trees. The earth grew to the size it is today and Sapling continued to create the animals. He would throw the earth into the air and the animals and creatures would form. He directed them to go in different directions and that they must go in flocks or groups. Some would take roost.

While Sapling was making the animals and seeing who would aid man, his brother Flint was watching and decided he could do the same. Flint made the body of a bird, as he knew it and when it was finished it flew, after a fashion. It flew about seemingly without any objective point—it was not a bird but what we know as a bat.

After making the animals, Sapling wandered the earth but didn't see any of the animals that he made. He stopped, wondering where they were, and heard a leaf rustle and saw a little Deer mouse. The Deer mouse, pleading for his life, offered to tell Sapling where the animals were. The Deer mouse said that the animals were in the direction of the great mountain range. He said when Sapling arrived he would find a large stone covering the mouth of a cave where the animals were kept by Flint and his grandmother. Sapling reached the cave and removed the stone to free the animals and told them that they were made to roam, not be kept penned up. Flint and his grandmother ran to where Sapling was releasing the animals and tried to stop them. They again put the stones against the mouth of the cave so now the only animals we see on earth are the ones Sapling was able to free.

Sapling was again traveling to inspect the land when all of a sudden he was walking in darkness. He couldn't find Flint or the grandmother. He saw in the distance a light like the dawn and he knew that was where the sun was. The spider, the beaver, the otter, and the hare all accompanied him. When they arrived at the light source, they all did their part to free the sun; Sapling threw it up into the sky so that the sun could light the earth during the day. He then found the moon and cast it up into the night sky saying that in the future when people looked upon the moon they would call her Grandmother moon.

Sapling then formed the body of a man and a woman. Flint, who was watching, formed what he thought were human beings and told Sapling how he could do the same as his brother. But the creatures were not human beings; they had human faces but the bodies of monsters. Sapling told him he could not create humans and he must not continue. Flint insisted that he could and would not stop.

Sapling came upon Flint standing at the water's edge with a man and a woman as white as the foam on the water. But Flint could not bring life to them. Flint said his creations were more beautiful than those made by Sapling but acknowledged what Sapling said was true; he wasn't able to make the humans. They were no good lying there on the ground at the edge of the water. At Flint's request, Sapling breathed life into the man and the woman and instructed them to move about the earth.

Sapling caused the waters to flow in both directions at once so that man would not have a hard time in his travels. Flint came along and changed that so the rivers now flow in only one direction. Flint made the mountains inhospitable to man, with their rocky slopes and treacherous high cliffs. For every good thing that Sapling created, Flint countered with something contrary. The competition between the brothers continued.

Though they lived together in one lodge, each stayed on his side of the fire. They talked, and in one of their conversations Flint asked Sapling what he feared would kill him. As his father had instructed him, he answered honestly saying it was a weed called "it cuts a person" and the spike of the cattail that grows in the swamp. When asked the same question, Flint said he feared yellow flint and the horns of the deer.

So whenever Sapling was out walking about and saw the yellow flint he would pick it up and place it high out of the way, and he did the same when he saw deer antlers. When he returned to the lodge he built the fire using hickory and it burned hotly. The lodge, which had one higher side and one lower side, was their home, with Sapling living on the higher side and Flint on the lower.

When Flint returned, he immediately felt the intense heat of the fire, which caused pieces of flint to begin chipping off of his legs. He asked Sapling to dampen the fire with some bark but when he placed the bark on the fire, the fire continued to burn. Flint writhed in the heat and ran out to the marsh where he found the "it cuts a person" and returned, threatening to kill Sapling. As the two began to fight, Flint noticed that the stalk of "it cuts a person" had no effect on Sapling. He ran out to find a cattail and when he returned he started to attack Sapling with that, but again it did nothing to him.

The two fled the lodge with Flint running away and Sapling chasing him. They ran in all directions all over the earth. Whenever Sapling saw the yellow flint or a deer antler he would grab it and throw it at Flint. This continued for some time until Flint was eventually killed. It is said that the mountain ranges in the west is where Flint lies, his lifeless body extended, because that is where he fell. Now you will notice that the earth is not a flat plain, it is undulating and uneven. It has it's high and low places interspersed with mountain ranges and it is said that it was that way because when they were running about they would stop and fight each other. Thus it was in those places that the land rose bearing witness to their struggle.

Sapling, who had begun to wander the earth again, came upon a man and asked him what he was doing.

The man said that he was inspecting the earth that he had created. Sapling replied that it was he who had created the earth. He then said, "If you did create the earth then you could move that mountain range at our backs to our bodies. If you can do that then surely you have created the earth." The man began to beckon the mountain range but the mountain range remained where it was. Sapling said, "It has not moved so it is obvious that you did not create the earth." The man answered the challenge saying, "So if it's true that you made the earth then you bring the mountain range here to our bodies." Sapling agreed and asked the mountain range to move closer and then instructed the man to turn around and see the mountain range had moved. The man turned around and struck his nose on the rock face. As a result his nose became crooked.The man then said, "Yes, it was you that created the earth and if you will let me live here I will forever come to your aid and that of man." He was called Mask and also Grandfather. He was instructed to live in the west and to come when he was called upon to help with ceremonies. He was to watch over the bodies of man and also bring the thunder and lightning and the waters of summer. In addition, Sapling asked him to come and kill the large serpents that might threaten the humans and that would be the food upon which he would feed. Sapling instructed him to always be available and to protect the humans and the earth, and that is where the legend ends.

I shortened the story, as some versions can be over twenty-five pages. In this story we have learned of the marriage tradition of the corn bread with berries being offered to the guests. We have learned of always keeping some of the corn back to dry and use for seed, not eating it all. We have also learned that the "Mask" in our Haudenosaunee culture, which is called False Face Mask by historians and ethnographers, is not a trinket or art piece or something to be made fun of; it is a ceremonial mask. There are many more teachings too long to list. That is the Creation story or part of it, as told by J.N.B. Hewitt.

Names Astir

Alice M. Azure

An early version of this poem was close to being a rant against certain gatekeepers of Acadian genealogy who espoused an ironclad DNA approach to determining whether aboriginal ancestors— most likely Mi'kmaq—mattered in the early colonial period of old Acadie, or the northeastern Maritimes. After cooling down a bit, I realized that as far as I was concerned, my ancestors from the old Kespu'kwitk District of Nova Scotia had not forgotten me. It was they who were guiding me in the forensic work of piecing together oral history, genealogy charts and results of autosomal DNA testing. As a result, the revised "Names Astir" is more grounded in the reality I was experiencing in my long search for Acadian ancestral names— French as well as aboriginal. And I am blessed to be a member of like-minded Métis people—my wonderful cousins, Amerindian Ancestry Out of Mi'kma'ki.

Guided by ripped pieces of a map
and a lantern's light of family stories,
I have ventured into a forest of genealogy,
seeking forgotten family groves.

191

I have come to find the names of unknown ancestors
sprung from Mi'kmaq women and French explorers—
coureurs de bois to lordly *seigneurs*—
people who joined their knowledge
of woodland rhythms and trading business,
people who made Acadia thrive.

I pay attention to the forest's wardens
,the ones who know where to find the proofs
of marriage, birth, baptism or death—
census lists of families, cattle and land,
records of unwanted people shipped out to sea
during the cleansing of Acadians
from their farms around the Bay of Fundy.

Tree by tree, I discover names.
I place beside each ancestor
facts and records of existence
until the leaves begin to tremble
on branches twined around
the trunks of Boudreau, Pellerin—
Mius, d'Anzy and Surette,
Belliveau, Savoie and Doucet.

I pay attention to other experts
flooding these groves of genealogy—
scientists who explore DNA technology.
Some see this work as validation
of relatedness, which I understand first hand
but I keep hearing whispers
the Old Grandmothers' warnings:

Pay attention, pay attention to
the undertows.
Remember, remember
your past is more than genes.

I scramble for the cover of my trees,
stumble into dreams of pulsing light,
of voices singing
singing stars,
all my ancestors singing,
my Marie *aborigènes,* Marie *sauvages—*
les Acadiens from Lejeune and Pinet
to Babin and Pothier.
I rest, overjoyed to be under creation's road.

Dove and the Teratornis

Phyllis A. Fast

In Koyukon *traditions the spirits guide you to notice the world around you to give you warnings about mistakes you might be making or about to commit. For instance, a big mistake is to avoid chores you are expected to do for your elders. In "Dove and the Teratornis" the little girl is supposed to learn both obedience as well as watchfulness. Sometimes the elder isn't a good person. In fact, he or she could be hurtful. Dove should learn by observation to avoid the hurtful kind and likewise to be good to the elders who are in genuine need of a kind deed or thought. But what about criminals, people who are much worse than hurtful? I decided that the ancient teratornis was just the bird to warn a child about an equally ancient problem that children need to learn generation after generation.*

"I won't go!" Dove flared. "Let Grandfather take care of Grandmother today."

"It's your duty, my daughter. He's waiting. Go!"

Dove's grandfather shuffled impatiently and reached out to his granddaughter.

Two pairs of slitted eyes razed each other, and then one slowly turned away and met her grandfather's gaze. Her mother watched as Dove allowed herself to be lifted and carried down a rugged mountain path. Something happened on their trip down the mountain, something that Dove told her own daughters many years later.

Dove once lived somewhere near the crumbling eastern edge of the Laurentide Ice Shield now inhabited by Canadians. What is now ocean used to be open land, vast grassy plains, beautiful crystalline beaches, and frigid uplands. Humans held a low position on the food chain—more often prey than predator. Like the saber tooth tiger, some creatures of that era have dwindled to haunting memories. One such ghost is the giant teratornis, a predatory bird that found a comfortable niche around the grassy plains. Their talons were better suited for walking on broad, flat surfaces rather than curling around branches or rocks. With a wingspan exceeding the length of two tall men, the teratornis were strong enough to lift a child as small as Dove. Their raptorial beaks brought fear to everyone, although their legs, long and bare of feathers, tempted some to risk humor. Every child grew up knowing that if they behaved badly, a teratornis would sweep down to steal them from their families. It so happened that like time itself, the story of Dove and the Teratornis came to repeat itself generation after generation.

At six years of age Dove was good most of the time, but

whenever her mother told Dove to take something to her grandmother, Dove forgot. Dove's mother worried, but after all, Dove was still a little girl, still her father's favorite, and always good in every other detail. When night fell her father waited for her to return. To him it felt as if days passed. When morning came he searched without success. He wilted with misery. "She's gone," he moaned.

"Do you think one of *Them* got her?" murmured his wife, lifting her eyes upward, punctilious about never saying the word "Teratornis" aloud.

Her husband grimaced, whether at her silly superstitions or his own fear, even he couldn't have said. He lifted his chin in their usual form of silent agreement. "I saw one circling around the mountain peak this morning. I haven't seen it since."

Dove's mother shuddered. Teratornis only circled a peak in rare moments of family distress. They preferred the plains for hunting. She knew the giant birds blamed humans whenever they lost a child or a spouse. Everyone knew the teratornis mated for life and usually hunted in pairs. When a teratornis spouse died, the other sometimes mated again, but human mythology of that era imagined the teratornis widows and widowers as forever lamenting the loss of a deceased partner. Storytellers referred to the giant birds as Teratornis Husbands and Teratornis Wives rather than insulting them with words suggesting they lacked social skills. Stories helped people accept the existence of bad behavior, such as abandoning an elderly parent or, perhaps, accidentally killing a wife or husband. Dove's mother searched through her inventory of tales to find the one that best suited the loss of Dove. She had none. She shuddered again, sensing this was to become a new, even more harrowing tale of murder and deception than any had ever heard before. As she awaited news of her errant daughter, she imagined a storyline. Later, when time had safely blurred all the versions, Dove claimed the story as her own.

It began like this: One day a Teratornis Husband landed on the edge of his nest and nudged his wife with his beak. He was pleased with the human girl child he had brought back to her. The child was still alive and was delightfully shaped. He nudged his wife again, and again she did not respond. With a shock the Teratornis Husband realized that his beautiful wife was dead. He rolled her over and saw that someone had torn out her heart. Blood—his wife's blood—pooled under her limp feathers. Unable to comprehend what he saw before him, the Teratornis Husband began talking to his wife as if she still lived, as if her breastbone was not cracked and exposed to the raw elements of their mountain aerie. He talked to her still body until the sun began its descent behind the western peaks. Even then he found more to discuss—news that he was desperate to share with her, his dead Teratornis Wife.

Dove watched him from the side of the aerie. By then she no longer shivered with fear. Silent, determined, and protected by spirits, Dove had spent that day examining the cliff for a way to escape. Each time he brought up a new subject with his dead wife, the Teratornis Husband would step around her prone body in a graceful two-step dance and then stop for a while to talk.

Dove thought he was screaming, not talking. She couldn't understand the Teratornis Husband's language. She thought he was either witless or insane. Wisely, however, Dove made use of the moments he stopped to scream at his wife's dead body to sneak around the rocky ledge. By the time the sun was nearly gone, Dove found a narrow trail that led away from the cliff top and away from the vicious beak of the wild Teratornis Husband. Keeping the Teratornis Husband in sight, Dove crept over the edge and was nearly out of sight when she saw the red eyes of the giant birdman.

Shrieking even louder than before, the Teratornis Husband flapped toward her—but it was too late. The little girl was gone. He tried to reach her with his beak by bending over the cliff, but Dove was too far away. He tried to walk down the path, but he was far too bulky and he nearly fell over the brink. For a while the Teratornis Husband railed at her, accusing her in his language of terrible crimes against himself and his wife. Soon his accusations took on a life of their own, and he found himself screaming so that everyone could hear:

"You murderer! You killed my beloved wife!"

The words penetrated his mind as nothing else had done. Suddenly quiet, the Teratornis Husband turned toward his wife. His crazed eyes cleared, and in the last rays of the sun, he saw that she was truly dead. In silence, shocked, horrified silence, the Teratornis Husband stumbled backward, away from the crumpled, bloody form. Soon his feet found open air instead of rock, but the Teratornis Husband kept moving until he plummeted downward.

As he fell, his eyes met Dove's. Something passed between them. Without knowing how or why, the little girl realized the giant Teratornis Husband who had flown the open skies with such beauty and power would never open his wings again. Dove heard a thud, then the sounds of cracking wood as his body crashed atop a tree. By then day had slipped away and it was too dark to see. Dove pressed her small frame against the cliff edge. After a long while she realized there was nothing left to dread. Eventually Dove made her way down the cliff and back home. Eventually she explained what happened to her mother and father. All of them agreed to agree that Dove caused the trouble by neglecting her grandmother. From then on Dove became the best of caretakers almost all of the time. From then on Dove searched the skies for signs of the Teratornis Husband hoping, despite all thoughts to the contrary, that she would see him again.

Her misery about the giant bird's suicidal fall never left her, but eventually Dove grew up and married. Together, she and her husband had three daughters. When her mother grew feeble, Dove stopped by once in a while to help with cooking and cleaning. Eventually it took more than an occasional visit to feed and care for her mother and later for her aging father. One day Dove asked her oldest daughter, Cana, to stay with the old folks, but Cana protested. She was about to marry and had no spare time. So Dove asked her second daughter to stay with their elders, but her second daughter was no better than the first. Finally, Dove sent her third daughter, who stayed with the aging grandparents but did little to help. Dove took her vexations to her husband.

"You could stay with them yourself," suggested her husband of many years. "I can take care of myself." He turned away languidly, thinking that his grin, ever so slightly libidinous, was hidden by the beauty of the surrounding mountains.

Dove caught the look and realized that he was thinking about the pretty widow in the cave across the way. She snorted. "You are growing old yourself, my dear husband. It has taken all of my time to create this great wealth for you." She held up the lid to their larder, piled high with tidy rows of bundled dried kelp and bales of oat grass for stuffing and fires. "I can't leave our cave for all the work I must do—all for you." Dove stretched her lips to expose still-white teeth in a mocking smile.

Her husband admired the larder and smiled at her with an equally large array of mostly white teeth. "It's time to go hunting," he remarked, "you don't have enough deer meat in there. I'll be back by evening with a new supply of meat for you."

After years of withering wedlock Dove knew that half of the meat would fill the widow's larder and all of his body would fill the slut's bed before the end of the day. She protested. He abjured. Their voices rose into shrieks that rivaled those of the teratornis.

After a while, he tried a new approach. "Why don't you bring your parents to live here? Between us we can take care of them." His smile broadened as Dove's face flowed with moods of sweet surprise to foul-smelling rivulets of hatred. He arranged his smile into one of tender love well knowing that his offer would never blossom into a disagreeable reality for himself even if all the old people in the world moved into his cave.

"My beautiful Dove," he said while his hands explored her private areas with loving pressure, "Don't worry about a thing.

I'll speak with our dear Cana again. She will understand."

Dove murmured something in return, but her husband's probing fingers distracted them both. Somewhat later that afternoon her husband awoke from their cozy bed and looked for his daughter. He explained Dove's concerns.

"Why don't you and Mother take care of them?" Cana asked, voice cracking. Building a relationship with her future husband hadn't worked as well as she had imagined. Her fiancé didn't seem to want to remain near her for very long. Worse, his face darkened frightfully whenever she spoke to him. Cana tried to tell her mother about her fears over her impending marriage, but Dove had been impatient and waved her away. Bringing herself back to the present, Cana searched her father's face and realized that he could be equally unconcerned about his daughter's future.

"Why me, Father?" Cana wailed.

"Your mother took care of her grandmother," reasoned her father. "Now it's your turn to take care of your grandparents."

Cana glared at her father, remembering the story about Dove and the Teratornis Husband. "She didn't do her part very well," she snapped.

"You'll be much better at it than your mother was," said her father, smiling amiably, sensing victory.

Indeed, Cana eventually agreed to take her grandparents

into her home with her new husband. As it happened, her grandparents helped in many ways to ease Cana's burdens. As one baby after another entered her life, Cana was glad of their help. She was especially glad of their presence the day that her husband arrived home and without warning raged angrily at Cana over a trifling problem. His shouts gave way to silence when three sets of eyes turned on him, each revealing wrath far greater than his. None of them spoke about the matter, but Cana came to note that it was the last time she ever saw her husband scowl at her. From then on Cana made sure that her grandparents felt even more welcome and comfortable in her home. No one told Dove of the incident, so Dove assumed all credit unto herself for the gentle glow of peace that continued to bathe her oldest daughter. In that state of self-satisfied innocence, Dove spent many blissful afternoons with her daughter and parents.

For a while, life moved in a hazy, comfortable glow until one afternoon when Dove returned from Cana's home a bit earlier than usual. As soon as her left foot crossed the entryway into her own cave, she knew what her eyes would find. Heart pounding, she waited until her eyes adjusted to the gloom before forcing her right foot to follow the first. She was right! The widow from the cave across the ravine sprawled in Dove's very own bed with lax arms draped across Dove's husband.

My ermine blanket!

The widow's right foot was hooked under an edge of the soft fur. Dove's eyes took in every detail of her prized matrimonial blanket, her husband's only wedding gift to her. Dove's knees dissolved without warning. She fell heavily on the stone floor of the cave but her mind would not let her lose awareness. Dove sought oblivion, but something forced her to lift her head and breathe in slowly to gather all the scents of the stony enclosure. The smell of the widow's vaginal fluids on the tender ermine hide assailed Dove's mind and stomach. Dove turned to breathe fresh air, desperate for its calming force. The ermine would never be hers again. Dove's mouth contorted in a silent snarl.

Neither will they!

Dove fumbled for her favorite, very sharp, meat-slicing stone knife. The familiar shape of the knife slid into the cup of her hand. Its comfort produced a sense of order if not peace. Still content in each other's warmth, neither her husband nor the widow heard any of Dove's stumbling movements. Their contentment goaded her to blind fury. Dove rushed toward the dormant pair and slit her husband's age-puckered throat. She was about to do the same to the widow when the younger woman awoke and jerked herself free from her lover's limp arms. Terrified, she clambered away, scrambling on all fours.

Once out of reach, the widow screeched, "You murderer! You murderer! You murdered your own husband!" She ran until she reached the other side of the ravine and her own cave.

Dove stopped. Her body stopped moving. Her mind stopped thinking. She stared at the blood, the fouled bed and the remains of the man who had once claimed to love her. Dove heard a loud creaking. She dashed out of the cave. At the top of a broken tree she spotted a big teratornis, blood dripping from his curved beak. Lucidity, or what passed for it, silenced the buzzing in her head and brought Dove back in time to a perfectly formed memory of clinging to the edge of the cliff when her eyes locked with those of the Teratornis Husband. More than a memory, the vision allowed her to understand everything that the Teratornis Husband had said and done on that long ago day.

"You killed her," she whispered, "and blamed me. You killed your own wife even though you loved her, and now I've killed my own husband even though I once loved him beyond all else. It's as they say: I am no better than the raging teratornis!" Flinging herself on her bed, Dove gripped her husband's body and sobbed, "and now I must do as you did," she murmured.

In answer the giant bird lifted its immense wings and shrieked so loudly that Cana, nursing her youngest child in her own cave and in her own time on another part of the mountain, looked up in mild curiosity.

"Was that a teratornis?" she asked her grandmother.

Smiling vaguely, the old lady found that it suited everyone if she didn't try to hear much. Cana shrugged and continued with her life's endless work. In the morning Cana felt a peculiar urge to visit Dove at her cave instead of awaiting her mother's daily visit. That's when she found the blood-soaked body of her mother wrapped tightly around the equally ravaged corpse of her father. Even as Cana wept over the unexpected loss of both parents, a small but pleased voice inside the young woman congratulated her that she no longer had to undertake even more exhausting work for yet more elderly people. Shocked by her selfish thought, Cana stilled her sobbing and stared for a long moment at her parents' bodies. So abstracted was she that she didn't notice her oldest daughter until the child tugged at her elbow.

"Mama? What happened?"

Rousing herself, Cana knelt beside her daughter and slid an arm around the girl's slim shoulders. "Your grandparents have died, my dear," Cana murmured, hoping she would not have to explain it further.

"Isn't that the bad bird? Isn't that the bird in Grandmother's story?" The little girl pointed toward the sky.

A shadow darkened the soil beside them. Cana glanced

upward and felt a tingle at the base of her spine. A memory, long suppressed, sprang to mind about a berry-picking party. She and a friend had wandered to the far edge of the field where they found lush bushes of alpine blueberries. Because the shrubs hid them, a pair of older women failed to notice Cana or her friend. The women were hissing and laughing behind their hands. Cana attempted to ignore them until she heard one speak her mother's name.

"Didn't he buy Dove?"

"What?! You mean Dove's husband? Wasn't theirs a love match?"

Under the shadowy canopy of leaves, Cana and her friend pressed into each other, keen to hear every word, eager to hear it together.

"He traded two beaver pelts for Dove," the woman declared.

"He murdered his first wife, you know," the other woman said in a cracked voice.

"I heard he killed himself," returned the other.

"I guess that was a lie, too."

The memory faded when Cana felt her daughter's tug again. "Mama, didn't a teratornis steal Grandmother?"

"No, my daughter," Cana whispered, "Not exactly."

"Did she lie to us, Mama?"

"Lie?" Cana swallowed the hysteria that rose in her throat.

Glancing at her daughter's innocent face, she took a deep breath and tried to think of something worthy to explain away the many strange trails that led to this violent end. "Perhaps she didn't know the truth herself."

"But Mama. . ."

Cutting through her daughter's curiosity, Cana smiled reassuringly. "Come. Help me prepare Grandmother and Grandfather for their First Walk of Death so they can begin their lives as spirits."

I Am

Doris Seale

My dear friend Doris is slowly fading into a new word. She continues to fight for what is right and just but can no longer tell you what time or day it is, what she ate an hour ago or even if she ate at all today. Yet her sense of what is unjust is as strong as ever, it's not fading away like the other things in her life. She still knows when someone is lazy, disrespectful or just plain cruel. I'm sure she will take this strength and with all the dignity she can muster up walk into her new world. When MariJo asked me to get a poem from Doris for her new book I wondered how it would be possible and decided to put it in the hands of someone more powerful than me.

After a few days Doris called me to tell me the poem was ready. I went over to pick it up. It just came out like "swamp gas," she said. "I think this is the best one I've ever written," she continued. "Doris I think all the poems you have written are your best work," I told her. She smiled and quietly sat back down. Together we've been packing up her home, saying goodbye to the many things she cannot take with her. I've been listening to the old stories that are attached to every item she has to let go of. It's difficult, we cry and we laugh and in the mean time I just keep

remembering the stories. *I guess when it comes right down to the end*
I think that is all we have anyway—the stories that is. Keep writing.
—Judy Dow, January 2013

> I am.
> I am not a thing.
> I am.
> The water.
> The tree.
> The light.
> I am —
> the wind.
> That,
> that is nothing makes me.
> I am.
> I am.
> I am.
> I am.
> I am.
> I don't know what else it might be but —
> I am.

We Who Walk the Seven Ways

Terra Trevor

Aunt Lydia said there is no such thing as being part Indian. She said Native people didn't think like that. Anyhow, even before she told me I already knew, have known forever that the phrase is simply not used, and especially not by me.

Bill said it was important for me to know who I am, and not to let my skin color define me. Not to let it define the way other people perceived me when they didn't know my story. And although it seemed natural that Auntie would have been the one guiding me to walk the sacred hoop—the female cycles of life as it pertains to Native women within American Indian tradition—instead it was Bill. Because he led me to the women who would show me the path, and pick up where Auntie left off. But back then I didn't know any of this. I thought Bill was only teaching me to become a better writer.

Now the body that once contained Bill was laid out in front of me at the mortuary, under a gray wool blanket that matched his gray halo of hair. Seventy-two years of the woods and rivers ran in his knowledge. His bone black hands were folded across his chest, oval fingernails gently curved, and his toes pointed up.

The last time I saw Bill alive, before darting out the door I said, "See you next week." Bill called me back. His eyes locked into me. "I certainly hope we do have the chance to be together again," he said. His words came at me like mosquitoes buzzing. I didn't want to think about what he was saying and brushed it off, and pretended not to understand what he meant. Then Bill put his hand on my arm, "You have an old Indian inside you, you know that don't you?" I nodded my head yes, but I couldn't look him in the eye. It was one of those stark and intimate moments I wasn't comfortable with and didn't know in how to be present.

Now time, as I'd always known it, had collapsed around me, and was going in a circle, just like Aunt Lydia had always said it would.

It was the year I memorized everything. Moonlight falling on the tangle of morning glories in my backyard. The certain set to my oldest daughter's jaw. Her crow black hair gathered in a ponytail at the nape of her neck, loose strands falling in her face, and watching her tucking them behind one ear. My youngest daughter, brown skin tanned, rolling her too serious eyes while smearing on strawberry lip-gloss. My husband getting up at the first dim light, moving quietly in the dark house making coffee for us. Bill, growing willow shoot thin, coughing every few sentences while telling me his stories, and the way my son's black hair shone red in the sun, and the freckle on his right cheek. We were still in uncharted territory, but my eleven year-old son Jay, wasn't sick anymore.

It is medically proven that a mother who is raising a seriously ill child can age ten to fifteen years faster than her peer group of mothers who are raising healthy children. Perhaps this is why at age 42 I found my way into the elders› writing circle Bill led on Friday mornings in Summerland, at the little white building near the church on Lillie Avenue. The shiplap side structure sat atop a hill on land that once belonged wholly to the Indigenous Chumash people, surrounded by orange California poppies in the spring, and overlooked the ocean with the Channel Islands beyond.

In those book manuscript writing classes I began feeling the way I do after a Sweat Lodge Ceremony and I could hear my great grandma telling me her stories.

Within Bill's writing class I began to make close friendships with women who were in their seventies, eighties, and two women in their nineties; all published authors. I began to form deep relationships that began to take me much further than writing. After class we brought paper sack lunches to the park that looked out over the Pacific Ocean. Frequently the conversation centered on women's work, but not in the common thought or practice that takes place within Western society. They talked about women's roles and the sacredness and respect of women in the traditional way. But they didn't say it like that. It just flowed from their natural conversations about politics, or sweeping the porch, and hearing Spirit give them an idea and needing to go write it down. Whatever it was, it gave me goose bumps, like I had when Aunt Lydia told me her stories.

Auntie always reminded me to remember my dreams, and feel my feet growing up from the ground so that I would be able to find my path within the great circle in relation to how Indigenous people viewed the world. And according to Auntie that meant woman's work that led to our spiritual path; that it was equally important to be kind, to help and let other women follow their paths. The stories she told me spoke of the female cycles of life within the medicine world. But she never used those exact words. Instead she told me stories, the ones that guided Native children to understand there was a natural world and a spirit world, and places that connected the two, through which some could, if they were supposed to, move from one to the other. But when I was young I thought her stories were like fairy tales, and that she told me the Grandmother Spider story to keep my mind off all the teasing I got at school, being called spider, because our last name was Webb, and I had long skinny legs.

Auntie and I had grown up within a family where all of the women had known their great grandmothers, and our great grandmothers had known their great grandmothers. From her great grandmother Auntie learned how to dig Sweet Root from the ground. Yellowroot, lady's slipper—she knew all of them. "Time goes in a circle," she often told me. And everything that has ever happened, or ever will happen was going on all around me, always. I didn't understand. But as a kid I could feel roots beneath my feet reaching back or forward into an invisible place where time lived. I thought of it as one big swirling windy place, where all of the things that will happen in the future, and what happened before I was born, came together and had a meeting of sorts. I didn't know how, only that it did.

Her shoulders had bent as she grew older, but Auntie was straight as a young girl when she told me her stories. Her words came from far away and sounded like wind in the trees, like running water. Most of the time I didn't understand what she was telling me, I only knew that I needed to tuck her words into my heart for safe keeping. Later on, Auntie no longer told me her stories out loud, because she had passed into the spirit at age 90.

After joining in Bill's book writing classes, I found myself within a circle of forward thinking elders who were also back to the blanket women following the feminine ways within American Indian traditions, and they wanted to pass what they knew on to me. They were picking up where Auntie had left off.

But back then I wasn't ready to carry it all. I didn't even read the book Anne loaned me, *The Sacred Hoop: Recovering The Feminine In American Indian Traditions* by Paula Gunn Allen. This pioneering work, first published in 1986, documents American Indian traditions and the crucial role of women in these traditions.

Anne was a respected elder in our community, an established author, and a woman I admired because she was teaching me how to grow old in a beautiful way. Now, twenty years later, I can look back and see that Anne was giving me guidance so that I could find peace and have a smoother journey in my role of mother and householder and family anchor. I loved being a mother. But after so many years of hard, hard parenting and being the mother of a son with cancer, I was feeling pulled in that mother-way of wanting to focus on myself and my writing career.

What I didn't realize back then is that the lessons I was learning about the sacredness and respect of women in the traditional way and disciplines were taking root inside me. I was open to learning what came disguised as the disciplines of writing, because at the time that was all I wanted to learn. But

Spirit saw my need and found a way in, and gave me elders who were ready and had limited physical teaching time on this earth, and to show me that that the old ways are still our ways, even for urban Indians.

I was within a circle of women, young and old following what author Paula Gunn Allen describes as *The Seven Ways*. Ways for women that are as ancient as the human race. My teenage daughters were walking *The Way of the Daughter.* I was walking the *The Way of the Householder*, along with *The Way of the Mother*, moving towards *The Way of the Gatherer.* Anne, already having already completed the other cycles was walking *The Way of the Ritualists* and *The Way of the Teacher.* Anne, I would much later begin to understand, was walking a medicine path. The disciplines of the medicine woman's way include the ways of all women as well as those walking towards roles as advanced practioners or the medicine path. But Anne never used those words. Instead she lived her life as an example. She was wise enough to lend the impression that she was no different than any other old woman, and this is what drew me in.

We WhoWalk the Seven Ways is excerpted from a memoir in progress.

A Turtle Narrative and Climate Change

Denise Low

When a group of Ketoowah people (a band of the Tslagi or Cherokee) lived near a warm sea, they found an abundance of food. One of the delicacies was eggs from thousands of sea turtles who entered their cove each year. The great domed females dug nests on the sandy beach and laid troves of eggs. Then, exhausted, they lumbered back to the water, submerged themselves in the shallows, and swam back to sea. Before the turtle eggs hatched, people collected some of them for food. For a time, as Ketoowah people gathered eggs, fruit, roots and grain, and as they hunted and fished, they prospered.

One year the turtles returned as usual, but children followed the slow reptiles as they left their nests. They dared to climb on their backs even when turtles went back into the shallow water. When parents and grandparents saw this, they scolded them. They told their children to appreciate how turtles provide food with the sacrifice of unborn young. Disturbed turtles would not complete their nesting.

The children obeyed for a few days, but on the seventh day, not even the older children could resist the novelty of turtle rides. Before long, all competed against each other, to see who could ride the farthest on their mounts. They ventured into the deeper, darker water. Finally, all the children, even the youngest, were riding turtles beyond the safety of the cove.

It was an older brother who first realized they were too far adrift, and he began to cry out. Then all the children called to their parents. But the turtles, following their own instincts, ignored their distress and kept swimming.

A Ketoowah auntie came to the beach, saw the children scattered in the sea, and called other parents. Uncles and mothers and fathers swam into currents and rip tides, and some of them drowned. As night fell, the full moon rose, and from the sea cliffs, the last turtles could be seen as tiny specks on the horizon. Finally, the curve of the sky was empty.

Ketoowah families left that place and began a migration north, away from their memories of sorrow. (Adapted from a story told by Benny Smith)

At first hearing, this story appears to be folklore, but let me discuss ways it has serious implications for 21st century people who pursue survival. The account, simple enough for children, orients us to an alternative approach to natural resource management. Respect for the natural world, a value shared by most indigenous American peoples, is the most important lesson in this story. Practical examples of this respect appear in practices of Menominee Indian forestry in Wisconsin; Great Plains fire management; and California Mountain Maidu forestry. Let us follow the sea turtle parable, one of the oldest Cherokee stories (according to Benny Smith), into new times and places.

Literally, this is a moral allegory with lessons for small children: Mind your parents; competition brings danger; respect the animals and their ways. Other lessons are: loss of children is devastating and changes communities; children are our foremost priority. Also, it is an accurate tribal history: Ketoowah band people divided in the 17th century, and one group went into Mexico. The great leader Sequoyah died in 1845 as he was visiting this group. In addition to tying bands of Ketoowah people together, this story has literary drama and implications about cosmology, geography, ecology, and ethics. Most importantly, this text is memorable and has lasted through thousands of years.

Although this story is a specific Ketoowah text, its archetypes of Turtle and earth resonate with many American cultures. In eastern Indigenous American cultures, Grandmother Turtle is the earth itself and the female principle. Among Lenape (Delaware) people, Turtle Island is the refuge for the hero and Lenape people during the great Flood. For Iroquoian and

Cherokee people, Sky Woman falls from a hole in the first Sky World, and the only place to land is on a Turtle's back. Mayan people understand creation begins with the appearance of a Turtle's shell, the Earth (Freidel, Schele, Parker 65). Sky cannot be raised from the Earth Turtle until three world-sized hearth stones, known to us as stars in Orion's belt, are raised off Turtle's back by Sky spirit-forces. Only because of Sky separating from earth do we humans have space to exist. For Mayan people, a split in Turtle's carapace allowed room for maize to rise into being (Freidel, Schele, Parker). Whatever our narrative may be, we all ride on Turtle Island, and the turtle is a living being, now sometimes termed Gaia—the ecological term referring to earth as a living organism. Embedded within oral stories are ecological principles that can be communicated to children as well as adults.

These American narratives share the idea that the Creator can take animal form. Oscar Kawagley of the Yupik people in Alaska notes that this implies equality among humans and the other animals:

Our creation myths say that Raven is the creator. Some say that the creative force took the form of the Raven to make the world so that the Yupiaq will never think that they are above the creatures of the earth. (*Worldview* 16)

God is not abstract, nor are humans singled out to have

special prominence among life forms. Religious paradigms for Native people are land-based and inclusive of all created beings; these differ from European cosmologies, which organize religious thought around frameworks of timelines, monotheism, and hierarchies.

A cautionary aside: Many Native people's religions require privacy about creation accounts and cosmological models. I am presenting only more general information that has been made public. Because religious rights were not extended to U.S. Native people until passage of the Native American Religious Freedom Rights Act of 1978, many religious practices went underground. These underlie Indigenous American sovereignty and survivance. This care with cultural thought is an important method of Native survival or "survivance."

"Survivance" is the Native term adapted from the French by White Earth Ojibwa member Gerald Vizenor to connote secular and religious continuance. Vizenor uses "survivance" with the implication of an ongoing presence. Specifically, he writes: "Survivance, in the sense of native survivance, is more than survival, more than endurance or mere response; the stories of survivance are an active process" (15). Survivance implies balance in relationship to past, present and future. Communication is another piece of survivance.

I once asked my husband Thomas Weso, a member of the

Menominee Indian Nation of Wisconsin, what his best skill was, and although he is not a humble man nor is his Nation known for humility about their history or courage, he chose "survival" as his best asset. His nation, in the 1850s, went up the Wolf River during a hard winter and dared the U.S. Army to remove them. The army declined. They survived and kept their land, and Chief Oshkosh continues to be a Menominee hero of that survivance.

Survivance occurs in many forms. I remember my father's brief prayers before holiday meals thanking the Creator for "food for the good of our bodies." These were the only times I heard him pray. I pondered his explicit request from intangible spiritual forces for maintenance of our bodies, and so indirectly my father taught me food from the environment is not an entitlement.

For the Ketoowah people, their oral narratives, such as the sea turtle story, demonstrate clear-minded understanding of the interdependence of generations, species, and the physical elements. Each bioform has its own behaviors, like the turtles that swim and do not respond to crying children. The sea sustains life, but at the same time, humans can drown its waters. The nature of humans is to save and repeat experiences in the form of language. The primary audience for the turtle story is the younger generation of Ketoowah people, so they can learn to coexist successfully within their ecology. Older generations reflect on deeper levels of the narrative. Native cultures have urgency about cultural survivance because in one generation, all oral tradition knowledge can be lost. Many Native children sent to Christian boarding schools lost religious ceremonies, stories, and language. But when they did return home, elders still told children's stories with impunity. These survived.

Words themselves are a method for survivance. Words construct models of the cosmos; words describe landscape and skyscape and their sign systems; and words themselves, finally, have their own dynamic, real energy.

Connotations of words shape our beliefs. Words create attitudes: like the word "wilderness" suggests conflict. "Green pastures" suggest sustenance and well fed grazing animals, like California milk cows. "Garden" suggests enclosed, idealized landscapes. When Adam leaves the Garden of Eden, he goes to a less nurturing place where he must: "till the ground from whence he was taken" (Genesis III.23). "Ground" is not as appealing as a "garden." So words about the environment revise how we can think about it. Take, for example, Rachel Carson's chilling term: "Silent Spring." Or take these terms that mark shifts in thought and praxis: Globalization. Green power. Biodiversity. Biofilia. Natural Systems Agriculture. Archology— which is the combination of architecture and ecology. Even, in the commercial realm, General Electric has an ad campaign named "Ecomagination." Kiowa writer N. Scott Momaday, who won the 1969 Pulitzer in fiction, asserts how naming is central to creation when he says:

…when you bestow a name upon someone or something you at the same time invest it with being. It's not an idea, by the way, that's peculiar to Native American experience; it's a worldwide kind of idea, but it is certainly important in American Indian society. … this is where things begin—naming. (*Winged* 92)

The polyglot American dialect recombines stems and suffixes and prefixes as fast as it can to articulate current ideas. The proliferation of environmental language terms shows the growing communal understanding of how important it is to realize survivance. New terms denote new strategies, so wordsmiths are essential to communication and survival.

The sea turtle story is performance of Ketoowah survivance. Within language Native people resolve grief, they reflect, they plan survival activities, and they archive their communal knowledge for children. Indigenous American peoples have used words to survive as distinct nations within the United States for five-hundred years despite disease, mass killings, slavery, assimilationist federal policies, religious persecution, industrialization, modernization, urbanization, and commercialism. With words, Native peoples create an enduring narrative about children who rode turtles and never returned, yet, paradoxically, these disappearing children continue to live in our minds, even in this very moment.

Words and breath underlie concepts of Native survivance. For many Native peoples—and it is always dangerous to generalize, but I shall here because I am selecting commonalities—the essential underlying premise of the cosmos is unity. The star constellations and heavens, earth, the flora and fauna, air, fire, and water, and words that express the cosmology are one cloth. Images that dance in human consciousness also fall within this definition of reality.

Our reality depends on life, the first principle of spirit. All life has its discrete, unique spirit. As the air's oxygen interacts with every physical element, the idea of respiration also applies to objects that may be considered "inanimate." A breathed word is a living being. Kawagley writes: "For the Yupiaq, there was no need to separate the things of earth into living versus nonliving, or renewable versus nonrenewable. Doing so would essentially bifurcate and breach the concept of interconnectedness" (20). In another mode, American poet Theodore Enslin writes the same idea: "Rocks are alive, just at a different speed."

Kawagley further describes Yupik language as a unifying quicksilver of this connected reality as he writes:

[My native language] opens the doors to the quantum fields and to the morphic fields, which are streams of connections—

connections to a great consciousness, connections to our ancestors, connections to everything of the land, the flora, the fauna, and the place. And we give special names to the places because these serve as mnemonics to let us know just exactly who we are and where we are at…. (*Impact* 8)

Kawagley believes language comes from the landscape. Other beings in nature have their own procedures, and humans renegotiate their relationship to them each day.

Along with unity, then, is another concept, which is: Creation is unfinished. The cosmos is multidimensional and dynamic, not static, and humans are participant observers in the ongoing creation of the world. They shift as the world around them shifts. Kawagley posits this paradigm of the Yupik worldview as a balanced tetrahedral structure:

If we use the three corners of the base to represent the human being, nature, and spirituality respectively as elements in a common circle of life, we can see the apex as representing the worldview that overarches and unites the base elements of our existence. (*Worldview* 14).

Kawagley stresses that to maintain balance among all the realms, mindfulness is necessary, or "ongoing monitoring to ensure the balance" (*Worldview* 15). In this model humans are one pole of the structure, but they do not stand apart from other elements. They must constantly adjust to the other realms to avoid collapse and to sustain survivance. Constant attentiveness is needed because conditions shift constantly.

Native writers watch scientists as they find ways to probe and record previously unknown properties of physical reality. Literary critic Ellen Arnold connects Native writers' philosophical worldviews to dynamic scientific thought: "Native American writers are drawing parallels between ancient tribal worldviews and the worldviews suggested by the new sciences of wholeness—quantum, chaos, and complexity theories" (xi). Osage writer Carter Revard integrates technology into natural tropes as he writes:

How time dawned on mind and was beaded into language amazes me the way an orb-spider's web or computer chip does, or the dance of time and space and energy that patterned selves into my parents, who did not have me in mind, and into the four children and seven grandchildren who've so far surprised us. Amazing that a brief quivering of air can re-present such wonders, that little coded curves of ink on paper might set the same vibrations pulsing from a human mouth in Buck Creek, Oklahoma and from others in Singapore or some future meadow or unbuilt spaceship. (xi)

Nature is unified and dynamic. In addition, natural elements of landscape have their own texts. If Raven and other beings are co-creators of earth, then the "languages" or sign systems of animal behavior are prayerful. The landscape holds spiritual beings that can provide spiritual and physical survivance. Kawagley, a hunter and fisherman, describes how these activities tie him to the land: "For matters of survival, the Yupiaq found that it was necessary to learn much about their immediate landscape" (*Worldview* 20). The surroundings are a dynamic text of earth-based languages.

Native people who have lived on the American Turtle Island have learned to revere the land as they live from its resources. The earth is a mother, in reality, not in metaphor. And the holy land is here, under our feet. In addition to information about environment for hunting or farming or mining or water resource management, Native people develop sacred interactions with the natural world and record them in their ceremonial epics and dances.

Vine Deloria, Jr., describes four kinds of sacred sites in the landscape: "[First are] Places to which we attribute a sacredness, because the location is a site where, within our own history . . . something of great importance took place" (3). Gettysburg and Wounded Knee, South Dakota, are two examples of this first site. A second category is where "the sacred appeared in the lives of human beings" (4). An example of this would be Buffalo Gap in the Black Hills, and migration routes of Pueblo histories and ceremonies. A third category for Deloria is "places of inherent sacredness, sites that are Holy in and of themselves" (5). Devil's Tower or Rock Tree, as Momaday's Kiowa people know it, is such a site. And finally, he recognizes sites that involve "a process of continuous revelation and provide the people with the necessary information to enable them to maintain a balance in their relationships with the earth and other forms of life" (5). Such sacred sites are places of continuing revelations from God, through ceremonies that continue oral narratives. Native religious practice is located in specific American sites. Children learn about place as they learn survivance.

Native thought foregrounds a dynamic landscape, with humans seeking balance within its laws. As much as Native people are connected to land, they are also mobile. The Sea Turtle story ends with migration as a salve for grief and as a blueprint for adaptation to adversity. Native peoples' literature is filled with migration narratives.

Indeed, contact with Europeans brought pressures to move, but, this was not the first such event, according to Mervyn Tano, an Indigenous Hawaiian, "We know we came from Havaiki," and anthropologists place this near Indonesia, but this detail is not as important to Tano as causes: "Some of the times [we move] because of climate change, because rivers dry up, wells dry up" (*Impact*). Or "a more powerful tribe has come in and is desirous of the lands we have inhabited." In the book *The Way to Rainy Mountain,* Momaday describes the Kiowa migration from the upper Rockies to western Oklahoma. These stories of movement emphasize yet again the condition of change for human survivance. Ketoowah people keep alive stories of travels from southern beaches as well as the historic Trail of Tears. People move. Creation moves. Because of climate changes, more movement will occur. Language preserves these experiences, and storytellers retranslate knowledge about unity, ongoing creation, landscape, and migrations for future generations. Migration tales are psychological preparation— some migrations are internal acceptance of change more than physical movement—and effective transmission of knowledge is essential to our survivance.

Stories of the Ketoowah, Yupik, Diné, Delaware, Menominee, Kaw, Osage, Maidu, and other Indigenous American people teach unity. They teach creation as not a distant origin story, but rather a constant, unfolding process. The land under our feet is a storehouse of wisdom and also a great dance floor. Migration stories are journeys of geography and also of the soul. People survive through their observation of the earth and her language; and they survive through archiving of knowledge in poetry and other arts. Indigenous traditions value the dynamic, transformative power of old words and newly invented word constructions as they constantly adjust to the movement of time. Calling the poet back into Plato's Republic allows for language to become a vehicle of sustainability, not a frivolous luxury. We live within a sea of change, we depend on other life forms, and we survive only if our children and our earth survive. Photographs of dried remnants of old water courses on Mars are chilling and urgent. We must find ways to place our storytellers in strategic positions on Turtle Island as we address the next phase of our collective human survivance.

This is our American sea turtle story, while we mourn lost life. Like Ketoowah children who ignore ocean waters, we also are vulnerable, and New Orleans will always have the story of Hurricane Katrina connected to it. New York City knows the power of Hurricane Sandy. We will reflect on these tragedies for many generations, as we find a better way to bridge the gap between experts in scientific laboratories and the people who need their knowledge. We can turn to revolutionary poets and artists who envision new languages for survivance; we can re-visit Indigenous cultures that exist outside mainstream academy and persist. This is the time to look again at overlooked models of human and natural interrelationships before sea waters rise beyond the point of no return.

An earlier version of this essay was presented to "Native American Paradigms of Sustainability." Chico State University's Institute for Sustainable Development, Feb. 21, 2007.

Arnold, Ellen. "Worlds Into Words: The Technology of Language in Carter Revard's Poetry." *Studies in American Indian Literatures* Series 2, 15.1 (Spring 2003): 32-9.

Deloria, Vine, Jr. "Sacred Lands and Religious Freedom." 1994. Rpt. *The Sacred Land Reader,* eds. Marjorie Beggs and Christopher McLeod. La Honda

Kawagley, Angayuqaq Oscar. "Talk at Haskell Indian Nations University." *Proceedings*, Symposium Impact of Climate Change on Indigenous Peoples, June 19, 2006. Lawrence: Center for Remote Sensing of Ice Sheets, 2006.

-----. *A Yupiaq Worldview: A Pathway to Ecology and Spirit.* 2nd ed. Long Grove, IL: Waveland Press, 2006.

Momaday, N. Scott. "N. Scott Momaday." *Winged Words: American Indian Writers Speak.* Ed. Laura Coltelli. Lincoln, University of Nebraska Press, 1992.

-----. *The Way to Rainy Mountain.* Tucson: University of Arizona, 1969.

Revard, Carter. *An Eagle Nation.* Tucson: University of Arizona Press, 1993.

Smith, Benny. Public lecture. Haskell Indian Nations University, Lawrence, Kansas 2004.

Part Five

Pathways of Sacred Spaces and Spiritual Energies

The universe in which Indigenous peoples live is alive. Spiritual energies, whether felt, dreamed, seen, or experienced exist where the cosmic force of interconnectedness creates formations. Without these numinous energies there is no spiritual time, no sacred spaces, and no spiritual wisdom of universal wholeness to be gleaned. There exists an inseparable connection of the earth with its inhabitants. Sacred spaces subsist where memories of significant knowledge remain. They hold the energy of past thoughts, songs, prayers, celebrations, ceremonies, visions and dreams of all entities that have existed before us as well as those to come. These are spaces where spiritual time reaches into material time and reminds us we are not alone.

Although some are desecrated or neglected—or in constant threat of becoming so, thus changing the energies manifested—the universe has a way of renewing revered spiritual energy. More sacred spaces are being created every moment, alongside old spaces as well as in new dimensions.

We are instrumentally accountable in forming and reforming these by reverently and ritually relating.

The Spiritual Universe

Vine Deloria Jr.

There seems to be a reasonable number of Western scientists and thinkers who subscribe to the idea that the ultimate constituent of the universe is mind, or mind-stuff. Fred Alan Wolf, a physicist writing popular interpretative books on the new understanding of the universe, said: "Today our position is close to the one discovered by basic tribal peoples. The concept of universal energy in our language might be called the 'universal quantum wave function' or 'matter wave' or 'probability wave of quantum physics.' This 'wave' pervades everything, and like the universal energy, it resists objective discovery. It appears as a guiding influence in all that we observe."

"Perhaps it is the same thing as the 'clear light'—the all pervading consciousness without an object of Buddhist thought."1

David Foster, the English philosopher, agrees: "When physics is explored to its depths, one comes across a world of mathematics rather than a world of 'things.' Similarly, in modern biology we have seen that beyond biochemistry we come to a world of information and literary logic in the DNA, and if one wishes to enquire 'what is behind the DNA?' there is little choice but to propose a similar LOGOS. It would seem that the developments in biology are even more suggestive than those from physics in confirming that 'the stuff of the world is mind-stuff' for while only some of us can grasp a basic mathematical reality, we can all understand the nature of language."2

F. David Peat, another English philosopher, elaborates somewhat in echoing Wolf's and Foster's understanding of the mental/spiritual universe: The "fundamental symmetries and their structures have their origin in something *that is close to a pure intelligence which springs from an unknown creative source.* The ground out of which matter emerges is also the source for consciousness, and indeed, since these two orders are essentially indivisible, it may be expected that 'fundamental symmetries' play a role in the structure of consciousness as well."3 (Emphasis added)

Werner Heisenberg earlier suggested: "I think that on this point modern physics has definitely decided for Plato. For the smallest units of matter are in fact not physical objects in the ordinary sense of the word; they are forms, structures or—in Plato's sense—Ideas, which can be unambiguously spoken of only in the language of mathematics."4

Carl Gustav Jung once admitted: "The mana theory maintains that there is something like a widely distributed power in the external world that produces all those extraordinary effects.

Everything that exists acts, otherwise it would not be. It can be only by virtue of its inherent energy. Being is a field of force. The primitive idea of mana, as you can see, has in it the beginning of a crude theory of energy."5 Even scholars working with near death experiences find themselves aligning with the quantum universe. Filippo Liverziani, an Italian scholar said: "The spiritual dimension of the other side appears to be a world constituted solely by thought. Thought creates it, directly, without any instrumental mediation; and it is also thought that knows it, experiences it, directly, and without any mediation of bodily senses."6

The above thinkers, and many others not quoted here, are of the opinion that the world we think of as solidly physical is, in fact, a strange, indescribable "mind stuff" that provides the foundation for everything. Jeffrey Iverson, writing on the near death experience, speculates: "the universe might be composed of thought, which could explain how an observer might appear to interact with his experiment. If matter is a "frozen thought" in a universe composed of "mind-stuff" then almost anything is possible—including the paranormal."7 The idea that matter is frozen mind stuff should be sufficiently clear to enable us to speculate further.

The conclusions reached by contemporary physicists, biologists, and near death scholars are a result of a long, tedious path from the Greek atomists and philosophers, through the European struggles with the false mind/body dichotomy, to the achievements in physics during the twentieth century. As increasingly sophisticated instruments became available to scientists, enabling them to pierce into the depths of the atom and then to wave/particle conceptions, the intellectual movement has been away from a hard physical universe to the descriptions cited above. Present conceptions of the universe therefore reach a conclusion that seems to represent the cumulative wisdom of Western science.

We have already seen that tribal peoples observed the world around them and quickly concluded that it represented an energetic mind undergirding the physical world, its motions, and provided energy and life in everything that existed. This belief, as we have seen, is the starting point, not the conclusion. Assuming or intuiting mind as the dominant entity, would not the tribal peoples' questions vary substantially from the questions asked by the Western philosophers? Would they not seek to know more about the mind behind everything they saw, felt, and dreamed? A significant number of American Indian tribes did adopt the idea that the world was mind, and we should examine their beliefs in this respect.

John R. Swanton, the great anthropologist, writing about the Muskogee Indians, summarized their beliefs regarding the nature of the world:

The world and all that it contained were the products of mind and bore everywhere the marks of mind. Matter was not something which had given birth to mind, but something which had formerly been mind, something from which mind had withdrawn, was quiescent, and out of which it might again be roused. This mind was visibly manifested in the so-called "living things," as plants, and still more, animals. Nevertheless, latent within inorganic substance no less than in plants and animals, was mind in its highest form, i.e. human mind. This might come to the surface at any time but it did so particularly at the fasting warrior, the "knower," and the doctor. Indeed, the importance of these two last lay in their ability to penetrate to the human life within the mineral, plant, and animal value in ordering the lives of their fellow beings. Not that mind was attributed to one's individuality, but that it was recognized as everywhere of the same nature.8

The Omaha understanding is similar and provides an articulate summary of the beliefs and practices of many tribes:

An invisible and continuous life was believed to permeate all things, seen and unseen. This life manifests itself in two ways: First, *by causing to move—all motion, all actions of mind and body are because of this invisible life; second, by causing permanency of structure and form,* as in the rock; the physical features of the *landscape mountains, plains, streams, rivers, lakes, the animal and man.* This invisible life was also conceived of as being similar to the will power of which man is conscious within himself—a power by which things are brought to pass. Through this mysterious life and power all things are related to one another, and to man, the seen to the unseen, the dead to the living, a fragment of anything in its entirety. This invisible life and power was called Wakonda.9 (Emphasis added)

The Sioux, according to A. McG. Beede, "believed (with no thought of gainsay) in Spirit (*Woniya*), which is the author and source of 'force and energy' in all things, or rather persons, for the entire world, to them, consisted of persons. So fully did the Western Sioux conceive all things as actually being, fundamentally mind, intelligence, reason, spirit."10 And the Hopis, according to Frank Waters, begin their creation story: "first, they say, there was only the Creator, *Taiowa*. All else was endless space. There was no beginning and no end, no time, no shape, no life. Just an immeasurable void that had its beginning and end, time shape, and life in the mind of Taiowa, the Creative. Then he, the infinite, conceived the finite."11

Scientists may well quarrel with the tribal terminology and say that the Indians were simple creationists, and, in a rigid sense, that was true. However, they did not draw the same conclusions as did the Middle Eastern peoples. With no scriptures to limit their inquiry or narrow their conceptual universe, the tribal elders had the belief that "the peculiar gift of an animate or inanimate form can be transferred to man. The means by which this transference takes place is mysterious and pertains to Wakonda but is not the Wakonda."12 We know from the discussion of how medicine men came to be that this mysterious energy generally summoned them through the offices or intercession of other forms of life, and then, through dreams and visions, they obtained powers that were shared with other forms of life.

The Indians developed as comprehensive analysis of the nature of the world as has Western science, but the goals have been very different. Western science is based on Roger Bacon's command to pry nature's secrets from her, by torture, if nothing else. The medicine men sought additional alliances with other entities, and, according to some tribes, accumulated both spiritual powers and cumulative knowledge over several lifetimes. The Muskogees thought that much knowledge had been given at the beginning of the world, and this governed each kind of entity and its activities. "While these things [other entities] did, indeed, have certain characteristic appearances and activities which were 'Natural'—that is, the things normally expected from them—they owed these to a certain impression made upon them in the beginning of things, or at least at some time in the distant past, and it was not to be assumed that they were all the powers which such beings and objects—or, assuming the Indian point of view, we might say simple beings possessed."13

Delving further into the Muskogee understanding, they discovered, as did all tribes, that "The power could be invoked by the use of charms and the repetition of certain formulae. 'By a word' wonderful things could be accomplished; 'by a word' the entire world could be compressed into such a small space that the medicine man who was master of the word could encircle it in four steps. It was power of this kind which was imparted to medicines, yet the source of this power was after all the anthropomorphic powers, which, at the very beginning of things, declared what diseases were to be and also appointed the remedies to be employed in curing them."14

If we live in a world of spirit and the landscape and entities around us are really frozen thoughts, then, in a reverse fashion, from creation or manifestation as a physical being, spiritual gifts can easily change, enhance, or contract the actors and events in the physical universe. We have seen sometimes there was diagnosis of an illness and recommendations that a certain medicine man could heal the disease, and other times when the healer simply did one or two things and the healing took place. The physical did not and could not withstand the attention directed toward it by spiritual powers.

There were two ways the medicine men used that established and maintained the link between the spiritual and physical worlds. When they offered and burned tobacco, sweetgrass and sage, the spiritual world opened itself up to them. Equally powerful were the songs that the spirits gave them. I know of no story that did not have sacred songs as an essential element in invoking the spirits. Indeed, songs were to the medicine men what instruments are to Western scientists searching for a deeper knowledge of the world. As we have seen, sacred songs appear to be more powerful and are much faster in their application and effect. Smudging seems to be the preamble to what thereafter follows.

The compatibility of tribal beliefs and Platonic philosophy is astounding. Black Elk remembered, "Crazy Horse dreamed and went into the world where there is nothing but the spirit of all things. That is the real world that is behind this one, and everything we see here—is something like a shadow from that world."15 Identifying the substance of the universe, then, as the function of mind, Black Elk felt that whatever we do of a spiritual nature enhances the physical and increases our appreciation of it. Recalling his vision experience, he said: "When I looked into the cloud, only [the] grandfathers were beholding me and I could see the flaming rainbow there and the tipi and the whole vision I could see again. I looked at what I was doing and saw that I was making just exactly what I saw in the cloud. This on earth was like a shadow of that in the cloud."16

The substance of the universe is relationships, the symmetries and their structure, as Peat expressed it. Indians say, "We are all relatives." Modern physics seeks to uncover the final piece of the puzzle in its pursuit of Higgs boson, believing that in finding this elusive particle, they can completely describe the universe. Even if successful, they will have only completed the logical circle and described the physical universe which is, after all, merely a frozen thought. In their ceremonies, medicine men are able to change the world and present it with new paths to follow. By healing, predicting, and locating lost objects, they cancel out the determinism of the physical and create different worlds that are consonant with the activities and direction of the world behind appearances.

SPACE

Time and space were the defining concepts of the Western philosophical tradition from the Greek atomists until the mid-twentieth century, when we were able to split the atom and show that the Einstein formula $E = mc2$ described the substance of the universe. These concepts were believed to represent absolute entities in the composition of the universe.

In Newtonian terms, they represented a structured universe and were dependable in that they always formed the context within which everything else happened. With the discoveries in subatomic physics, we learned that they merged together and became useless when describing miniscule atomic events. Today, they are regarded as flexible concepts, useful in a human-sized world, but increasingly mysterious at macro and micro levels of inquiry.

Space is found in most tribal traditions, hidden within ceremonies, but certainly occupying a critical place in helping to orient us to our sensory world. The Plains Indians, in beginning a ceremony, always point their pipes to the six directions: up, down, north, south, east, and west. This ritual pays respect to the powers of the universe, and recognizes that they appear to us as a group of powers and center our emotional universe for the purpose of communing with the spirits. The sweat lodge is built in the shape of a sphere and reproduces, as closely as possible, the cosmos as a whole. The sand paintings also represent the universe, and to avoid being trapped within the powers that the paintings summon, the work is never finished, and a little lapse in the continuity of the drawings is left. The spirit lodge has a unique feature in that it is an elongated version of the cosmos and provides a forum within which we can communicate with the spirits.

The power of space is one of relationships, and since the entire cosmos cannot be contained in our daily lives, we learn that sacred places represent the power by showing us that we can become a part of a preexisting set of relationships. Each tribe has its own center and its own boundaries marked out by reference to existing landscape features. Thus some Plains tribes say that Pikes Peak in Colorado is the center of the universe, but Rainy Mountain or Harney Peak are the center of their particular universes. When people accommodate themselves to a landscape, they learn the parameters of their spiritual existence, although sometimes these boundaries change according to the needs of the people. Thus a good number of tribes saw the Pipestone Quarry or the Bear's Lodge (Devils Tower) as part of their universe, even though they were not centrally located. One might, indeed, draw a map with inconsistent and overlapping boundaries to illustrate the economic, political, social, and religious worlds of each tribe.

One final example might be how space changes to accommodate the spiritual energy that can be mustered in a ceremony. We have no examples of this phenomenon, but only the undocumented statements of medicine men as to their experiences. The Lakota tradition says that there is another world beneath the Bear's Lodge with trees, lakes, and prairies. It can be entered only by certain people who have this power.

The popular name for these locations is the portal between worlds. In the Cheyenne tradition, Bear Butte is such a spot. It is where Sweet Medicine received his revelation and the sacred arrows that guided the people for thousands of years. There is no cave at Bear Butte—except for the one into which the medicine men can enter.

The Pawnees have identified a number of buttes in Nebraska that are, in fact, animal lodges where the animals and spirits of animals reside. We have already seen the immense powers of the men of this tribe, and one power reported—but not in written sources—is that of transforming themselves into their animal spirits. Walter Echohawk, a prominent Pawnee elder, said that when Quahnah Parker came to visit his tribe and sought permission to speak to the doctors in the sacred lodge, they greeted him in their animal form.

William K. Powers discussed the practice of the Sioux in calling upon all the powers of the universe. In this procedure, sacred space is created. "When an Oglala wants to call upon all the types of *sicun* in the universe he must prepare one tobacco offering for each of them. Each tobacco offering, called *canli wapahte* 'tobacco bundle,' is made from a one-inch square of cotton cloth into which a minute pinch of tobacco has been placed; the cloth is shaped into a small ball and tied to one string. During certain rituals such as the vision quest and

Yuqipi, all 405 tobacco offerings are tied to one string that is used to delineate a sacred area metaphorically called the *hocoka.* Hocoka is an old word that refers to the inner part of a camp circle, but as used ritually it means a sacred space, the center of the universe, within which a sacred person or suppliant prays, sings, or otherwise communicates with spirits."17

In summary, then, space is critical to the Indian perception of the world, but primarily because it can be created by the holy people, and energies and information can be transported from the larger cosmos to the particular location where humans need help and sustenance. If other religious traditions have a similar idea of space, their beliefs have not been articulated or communicated.

1 Fred Allan Wolf, *The Dreaming Universe: A Mind-Expanding Journey into the Realm Where Psyche and Physics Meet* (New York: Simon & Schuster, 1994), 206.

2 David Foster, *The Philosophical Scientists* (New York: Dorest Press, 1985.), 169.

3 F. David Peat, Synchronicity: *The Bridge Between Matter and Mind* (New York: Bantam Books, 1987), 196.

4 Werner Heisenberg, *Across the Frontiers* (New York: Harper & Row, 1974), 116.

5 Carl Gustav Jung, *Civilization in Transition* (Princeton, N.J.: Princeton University Press, 1975), 69.

6 Filippo Liverziani, *Life, Death and Consciousness: Experiences Near and After Death* (England: Prism Press, 1991), 151.

7 Jeffrey Iverson, *In Search of the Dead: A Scientific Investigation of Evidence for Life after Death* (San Francisco: HarperCollins, 1992), ix.

8 Swanton, John R. "Tokuli of Tulsa, in Parsons," American Indian Life, ed. Elsie Clews (Lincoln: University of Nebraska Press, 1922), 142.

9 Fletcher and La Flesche, *The Omaha Tribe*, 134.

10 Beede, *Western Sioux Cosmology*, 2.

11 Waters, Frank, *Book of the Hopi: The First Revelation of the Hopi's Historical and Religious Worldview of Life* (New York: Viking Press, 1963), 3.

12 Irwin, *The Dream Seekers*, 70.

13 Swanton, *Social Organization and Social Usages of the Indians of the Creek Confederacy*, Smithsonian Institution, Bureau of American Ethnology (Washington, D.C.: Government Printing Office: 1928), 189.

14 Swanton, *American Indian Life*, 143

15 Neihardt, *Black Elk Speaks*, 85.

16 DeMallie, *The Sixth Grandfather*, 215.

17 Powers, William K., *Vision and Experience in Oglala Ritual* (Lincoln: University of Nebraska Press, 1984), 29.

The above is excerpted from *The World We Used to Live In: Remembering the Powers of the Medicine Men*, Fulcrum Publishing © 2006 Vine Deloria Jr. Printed here with permission of the publisher. (Thank you, Sam Scinta.)

In the Country of the Wanderer's Hand

Jim Stevens

"Country" is the last poem of a forthcoming collection centering on my 40-year relationship with a sacred site deep in southeastern Wisconsin's kettle moraine region. Popularly known as Aztalan, the town was closely in tune with the stars, both in time and geography. This alone would mark its place as an important cultural center.

Aztalan was certainly not the name of the town, which was surrounded by a wall, which formed the likeness of a horse. I have learned to call this ancient community Big Dog Town. This refers to the literal meaning of the Hochunk word for the creature. As goes the legend, big-dogs were dream helpers. There is a hill in present-day Madison, which was dedicated to their spirit.

At Big Dog Town there was a Longhouse, and this would have been common in our northern region. But I have come to consider that Big Dog Town was something of a small international center, for it appears that a Roundhouse (a Kiva) was situated along the river fronting the town. There were also two types of houses in the community, one rectangular, the other circular, in the form of a "G."

Still present just south of the town walls is a standing stone. In its ancientness, it connects the town with some springs, and then slightly further to the east across the river, an enormous Water-spirit mound. This flow of energy anchored the town to the Otherworld. The continuing presence of the Water-spirits was manifested for me one day when I found that in a certain light, lichen of the stone displayed the unmistakable forms of these legendary creatures. For this we can certainly thank the Little People, once and future co-founders of this ancient system. They dance all night at their stomp circles, far into the Deep Field.

The one who struck a rock and the water flowed out
Has lived with the mystery of earth and her consorts
He is to be seen there when the sun is at its height
Sitting on the hump of upright stone to tell the story
Across the grand blue-stem from seven water-spirits
For deep the music came and stark as the life
Of the wind from where the flowers burst
And they grew within the shadow where his feet trod
A lunar quilt whose presence at the center of the roundhouse
Leapt startling into the dance of the trees
Spirits of horses dreaming their way into the clouds
It was the way the shadows of the city took form
Their mythic drumbeats coming along with the rain

Waiting for the light-bodies from across the river
They come and go in a flash from the deepest sun
Flowing with the rivers at the foot of the high ground
For this is forever the home of the story
And the one who had his birth here
Was finding his way into the grove of slender white trees
Where the dark skin of doorway caused his heart fullness
When the silver moon was a great body along the prairie
And it was strange to find so many souls in the grass
Glimmering with the air and holding silent
Across the distance and winding into the world
When he was the first creature to pass this way

the geo-physics
of de-tribalization

ire'ne lara silva

This poem was inspired by a writing prompt from J. Michael Martinez during CantoMundo 2011. It gave me the perfect format to articulate something I'd wanted to write about for a long time in a way that was more descriptive than a list, but more condensed than a long essay. This poem chronicles the large movements of history and loss, grief and destruction and how I feel—as part of a communal body—the loss of a communal name and a way of life. However, this is also a poem for laying claim to what I feel and know in my body, absolutely and unwaveringly: that I and others of us who are de-tribalized, do belong to this land.

table of contents
Chapter 1. *Hurricanes:* counter-clockwise winds
of disruption, more than
five hundred years of category 5 storms,
all of them named *Massacre*
named *Betrayal* named *Stolen*
named *Genocide*

Chapter 2. *Drought:* only our ancestors' blood poured
onto the cracked earth, everything green dying,
violence and screaming,
and the smashed skulls of infants
laying bleached under the sun

Chapter 3. *Wildfires:* disease, the land stolen as the fires
of smallpox and influenza, bubonic and pneumonic plagues,
raged in every direction, leaping wildly,
as they added blankets to fuel the roaring,
leaving charred bodies in a ravaged landscape

Chapter 4. *Tornadoes:* piercing cyclones between their thighs,
the rape of their dark-skinned flesh,
blood and weeping, invading seeds,
wombs straining in the wake
of a war without name

Chapter 5. *Volcanoes:* molten earth rising, orange and red
lightning splitting the dark skies, the ash of colonization
smothering histories and libraries
and human bodies

Chapter 6. *Earthquakes:* vehement earth, injured earth, ruptured earth, lands come undone, millions disappeared, nations forced from their lands, nations scattered
even the clouds wept

Chapter 7. *Floods:* raging waters of amnesia which ripped away all of our stories, leaving families, communities, nations like broken-limbed debris

Chapter 8. *Sinkholes:* erosion of our names and our languages, cataclysms of forgetting, shadowed caves of shame, collapses which rendered us unrecognizable

Chapter 9: *Magnetic fields:* we are the children, electric in our waiting, inexorably pulling us to each other, recognizing no distinctions in time

Chapter 10. *Deep ocean currents:* under the surface of the ocean, hidden and immense, returning, rising,
writing our names on the sand
we may be de-tribalized
but we are still indigenous to this land
we still belong

After Sayra Tagged Me with a Facebook Picture of Chief Raoni Weeping over Brazil's President Approving the Belo Dam Project on Xingu Land (for Sayra Pinto, Mayan Poet)

Susan Deer Cloud

This poem came to me in one long flash of sorrow and remembrance. I suppose all too many people believe that the stealing of Indigenous lands and physical and cultural genocide have ended, but this is not true. The genocide continues. When I read about Chief Raoni's weeping, I also wept. I grew up in the Catskill Mountains and return there frequently and now may be able to go back for good. All that the physicists are saying about the universe is not news to me. My elders raised me in a dreamscape of understanding that everything is interconnected and that clock time is a human invention. I grew up surrounded by birds and animals, lakes and rivers, forests and meadows. I walked wrapped in the shawl of story, poetry and song

263

fringed with eternity. I know how bereft Chief Raoni and I and other people feel when they lose what I call "heart country." The irony is that my mother told me not to tell outsiders about our beliefs because they would think me crazy. The justice is that physicists and other scientists now speak like a bunch of "crazy" Indians, poets and mystics. The beauty is that I am laughing until my tears flow like un-dammed rivers sparkling in moonlight.

I was thinking about Chief Raoni
yesterday when I drove into my
beloved Catskills on the way
back to the Southern Tier (Tear) ....
what so-called "progress" means to
those who love their part of Mother
Earth in a way that the rootless
don't ever understand...

... Of course, I don't own
the land ... no one owns it, really ...
only more and more of mountains
bleed bright orange-red posters
on trees... so I can't wander
parts of that country anymore
unless I sneak onto it and don't

get caught. Maybe there are
those of you who remember
how it was when you could
wander freely and dance
on Earth and not worry
about barbed wire fences,
electric fences, and the bleeds
of posters warning KEEP OFF.

I spotted two deer near old apple trees
along Elm Hollow Road. One
a yearling doe, one a spike horn.
I stopped Purple Wampum Pony
(my old car), rolled down window
and softly spoke to doe and buck...
watching ears flick back
and forth... watching them wonder
if they need fear me who appears
like the pale shadows who strung the fences ...
smiling at those deer trespassing
on posted land... their silence, my
soft voice... my silence when
they leaped into the rain music
of September woods.

I took photographs of
Elm Hollow Road and old road
along Beaverkill River... in rain,
in mists... land I call
heart country... land
where my heart song began.
One of my biggest fears?
That anyone would ever blast
off tops of Catskill Mountains
as men have done in West Virginia
and Illinois... to me
unbearable.
What if the future has
nothing left of the mountaintops
except photographs such as mine?

What if the future mechanically
combs the twigs and leaves
out of wind-braided hair?
What if the future has no more
two-leggeds like me ... no
wisdom-haired elders old enough
to remember rambling freely
among elms, the turning

leaves and unfenced
woodlands, lakes and creeks?
What if the birds …
the other two leggeds …
cease singing because there flame
no more trees?

What if the future loses her memory?
What if she even forgets
how to weep the way
Chief Raoni cried over
his people's rainforest lost forever
to the "progress" of fencing
in freedom and flooding all
the Beauty Ways?

Directions

Odilia Galván Rodríguez

This small poem series is in keeping with the Mexica [Aztec], tradition of preserving for future, the ancestors' voices through the sharing of poetry and song—Flor y Canto, or literally, "flower and song." If we honor ancestors they honor us by helping us to tap into the legacy of the peoples power and healing, passed down through the ages through our stories, celebrations, and ceremonies despite much adversity. I believe that we can even re-member lost traditions if we are open enough and listen. Tlazocamati (Thanks)!

a moon was birthed in a purple
sea, almost one month before the end
of the *b'ak'tun*,* that was finally moving
on, and some worried it was really
"The End" they believed prophesied in codices
by ancient ancestors who were not theirs
and they chose to believe, without listening...

she gathers the memories of her family
in old vision baskets woven water tight
though she can not see the future,

she hears the ancestors, they too talk
of past times that have moved on
often their sharp tongues cut through lies
ones a family tell themselves to survive

embracing the storm she took two knives
from the kitchen drawer and walked slow
to the front door of her home,
fashioned from an old recycled railroad car,
she ordered her grandkids, under the beds
through open door she saw thunder beings
with crossed knives she spoke their language

large land masses broken and split off
from their traditional geography, landmarks now gone
a longtime peoples homes and history divided
from what was once truth for centuries
time moves on but their ghosts remain
crossing this land they always belonged to
these directions sacred never will be forgotten

an ochre pony leads the whole pack
a wild bunch they're never going back
into a captivity where they were broken

artificial life with so many horrors unspoken
horses were born to roam the prairies
where they shall gallop fearless and free
carrying only worthy warriors on their backs

* *b'ak'tun* is 20 *katun* cycles of the ancient Maya Long Count Calendar. It contains 144,000 days, equal to 394.26 solar years.

The Next Page-Turner

Tiokasin Ghosthorse

Something different has happened here on Turtle Island and only some have noticed it. Others have run away with it to a point of no return because they've individualized it. Others have intellectualized it with the same paradigmatic thinking being forced upon us for the last 41.66667 decades. We seem to blind ourselves with the "new awareness" and fait accompli *without including the necessity of knowing who we are and getting lost in the idea of becoming something. So my thoughts are these…*

What do I say to a crowd like this? Do I say welcome to the list of insecurity? Do I say something that might upset you and jeopardize your comfort zone? Do I say something like welcome to our country? Let me remind you of a Native way of thinking. We have no word for exclusion, but for inclusion. We come into this dimension as energy, and what we do with that energy dialectically while we are in this program is what matters in the end of this dimension. We enter this dimension without labels or price tags and return to that pure energy, but it has been a world exacting it and returning nothing. I ask you all to take down your walls, your factions, your democracy, your socialism or whatever label. I say:

In order for Mother Earth to continue to live
Men have to give up their male ego and admit that the religions,
the politics the patriarchy in general is at the fault
We must turn our machismos into the fodder that it is and let the
seeds grow in the manner that the Creator intended
We must relearn how to be men in a non-patronizing manner …
in a non-matronizing manner so there remains a balance
A place where nobody hides their hearts
In this illusion there is nothing to compare it to
In the world where there flies no flags of any "-ocracies or isms".

The French anthropologist Claude Levi-Strauss found an Indigenous people in South America some forty years ago, who claimed to see Venus in the daytime. When this seemed impossible to him, he conferred with astronomers who verified the fact Venus does emit enough light to be visibly seen during the daylight hours, but only to highly trained human eyes.

I think we are here to provide a generativity of trust as caregivers, not caretakers, and for all this "new awareness" there lacks a tolerance and how profoundly diverse Native cultures are from the dominant culture surrounding us. These distinctions create very different attitudes toward Mother Earth and these differences make it more crucial in accepting the perspective of how to survive the ecocide system created by the dominant culture. The dominant culture's anthropocentric values are placed away from the prescient values of Native cultures by experimentation and not the familiarity of living it. The dominant culture that has forgotten its intimacy with Mother Earth for a long, long time—the longer the time the harder it is to remember. So it is with the dominant culture›s war against Mother Earth and its stepped-up intensity and depleted sense of integrity with its own origins or denial of it.

This is not about comparisons but the differences.

Become the warrior that we have expected you to be. This is your responsibility. Our bodies are in the soul and that soul is your responsibility. We must use the energy respectfully. Some of you disagree. I disagree with a system that is an enemy to the natural world. The next move is yours. *Mitakuye Oyasin* (We are all related = E=MC2).

Tsankawi's Trail

Tony Abeyta

Tsankawi* is a place where spirits of past and present parallel infinitely.

I speak of that place, where the earth erupted. It's now hardened coral and cream colored ash in its ribbon patterns of soft sediment. That place where the scientists have now built their secretive laboratories of Los Alamos on the edges of cliffs and then into their mysterious canyons, hidden from our curiously suspicious eyes. From this vantage point, I can see the whole pueblo world below and beyond. There...I see that serpentine, River that emerges from a dark canyon to the north, only to name the new, expansive valley for its very own.

The Navajo call this our glittering world. I know this now... as I grab a handful of those tiny transparent crystals from the powdery ashen trail at my feet. They are all gently strewn throughout this sunlit summit, all to contemplate—to arouse inspiration and to remind me of those carefully selected stone granules atop an ants' pile. The ants remember each one, on their daily journey into their underground where these crystals all once emerged. Deep within their cool and earthen tunnels, they continue to mine their selections of colorful and translucent gravels, as they have for thousands of years.

I continue my own meandering journey, knowing that my time is ending as winter approaches, and I must now leave, as the air turns colder. I follow this trail as many have for hundreds of years, instinctually remembering their exact rhythmic, pace of foot pattern upon this path. I stop, and smile, as I look skyward, knowing that night will come and echo in this constellation, an equally random display of shimmering stars upon that deep and absorbent blackness. Those are the stars that will surely recognize their likeness on these sacred grounds. Look, as this array pulsates and shimmers all in unison, above and below. This moon's light reflects back and with its sliver of a smile, It remembers that it all changes so quickly. It knows, that we as a people, come and go and leave our ephemeral trails, then…all the rest will magically stay the same.

*Tsankawi, pronounced "sank-ah-WEE" is also known as *saikewikwaje onwikege* meaning "village between two canyons at the clump of sharp, round cacti" in Tewa, the traditional language of San Ildefonso Pueblo, New Mexico. Ancient Pueblo Indians sometimes known as the *Anasazi* built *Tsankawi*. Archeological evidence indicates that *Tsankawi* may have been constructed in the 1400s A.D. and occupied until the late 16th century.

Among the Stars

MariJo Moore

Various Mayan elders have encouraged their people to go to the sacred sites and perform rituals in order to "take in the knowledge of the sun." By doing this, the Maya hope to understand what they have in their memories and use this knowledge to wake up society as to the environmental damage being wrought on earth.

Some Hopi elders have said that if just one person continues to practice traditional ways, there is hope that the energies deeply entwined in the universe will continue balancing. I am determined to remain positive and believe there are those who do want to stop the senseless abuse and neglect of others and this planet. For those who let material gain and greed rule their lives, perhaps something will cause a great change in their patterns of thought. After all, time is definitely a circle that guarantees what goes around comes around.

When all secret thoughts of the universe are known,
life will begin again.
When dark waters breathe into the bluing mouth of the sky,
when all that sprouts from the blazing core
is singed in harmonious change,

when masculine and feminine energies are equally accepted,
when time crawls inside itself, exposing eternal existence,
then all shall know there is, always has been,
everlastingly will be
a Sacred Place where spirits gather to pray for all in all.
Let us become consciously, ceremoniously grateful.

Contributors

Tony Abeyta was raised in Gallup, N.M. of Navajo and Anglo descent. He creates a powerful range of contemporary paintings. He explores different mediums such as oil and monotype creating a variety of pieces including charcoal drawings, large-scale oil and sand paintings, and abstract mixed media pieces incorporating encaustic wax, copper and printmaking. His individual style incorporates bold colors, rich textures and representations of Navajo deities. He has presented numerous art exhibitions and his work is in various museums as well as selected private collections. He resides in Santa Fe, NM. tonyabeytastudio.com

Alice Azure's writings have appeared in a number of journals and anthologies such as *The Mi'kmaq Anthology, Volume Two: In Celebration of the Life of Rita Joe; the Florida Review*; and *Yukhika-latuhse*. She launched two books in 2011—*Along Came a Spider* by Bowman Books (a memoir), and a chapbook of poems—*Games of Transformation* by Albatross Press—the latter selected as the poetry book of the year by Wordcraft Circle of Native Writers & Storytellers. She earned an M.A. degree in urban and regional planning from the University of Iowa and is recently retired after twenty-five years of service in the United Way movement. A Mi'kmaq Métis, her roots are in the Kespu'kwitk District (Yarmouth) of Nova Scotia. She lives on the Illinois side of the St. Louis metropolitan area and is a member of the St. Louis Poetry Center.

Carol Willette Bachofner, currently Poet Laureate of Rockland, Maine is of Abenaki descent. She often writes from a perspective of that culture which underlies her poetic impulse. Bachofner is an editor, publisher, blogger, teacher and mentor of other writers. Her poems are widely published in such notable journals as, *My Home as I Remember, The Comstock Review,* Prairie *Schooner, CT Review, Main Street Rag, The Cream City Review, Crab Orchard Review*, and others. Nine of her poems will appear in the forthcoming *Dawnland Voices: An Anthology of Indigenous Writing from New England* (University of Nebraska, ed. Siobhan Senier). Bachofner is the author of four books of poetry: *Daughter of the Ardennes Forest, a PTSD WWII Memoir; Breakfast at the Brass Compass, poems of Midcoast Maine; I Write in the Greenhouse;* and *Native Moons, Native Days.*

Sidney Cook Bad Moccasin, III (born April 19th, 1979) is an enrolled member of the Rosebud Sioux Tribe from the Burnt Thigh Lakota Nation in South Dakota. His talented gift as a motivational speaker is geared toward shedding light on ignorance and to uplift and inspire individuals to reach their full potential as human beings and educating the public about Lakota and Indigenous value system. Bad Moccasin's primary focus is addressing low self worth among Native American youth and suicide, drug and alcohol abuse prevention and recovery, strengthening spirituality and self esteem in Native American youth. Bad Moccasin is currently the owner of Parfleche Designs by Sid Bad Moccasin and Bad Moccasin Consultation providing traditional Lakota art techniques and lectures to intrigued individuals worldwide about the rich and diverse Lakoka culture. He resides in Pierre, South Dakota. http://www.facebook.com/sidney.badmoccasin

John D. Berry, M.L.I.S., M.A., Native American Studies Librarian, U.C. Berkeley, is of Cherokee/Choctaw/Scots-Irish/German heritage. Son, husband, father, uncle, John has worked at Federal Libraries for the DoD and the FDA, and other academic libraries, as a field archeologist in the U.S., Israel, and the South Pacific, a machinist and a stage coach bandit. He is a master Mason and is listed on the Native American Authors pages of the Internet Public Library. Writings and poems may be found in print or on the web and have been translated into French for a literary journal from Paris, and also into Catalan on a Catalan language website. He is he author of *Artifacts* (Benicia, California, 2012), which includes photographs by Tora Williamson-Berry. "I'm not a Medicine person, or a traditional leader, only an average Indian guy, and I speak only from my perspective."

Duane BigEagle (Osage descent) has taught creative writing since 1976 with the California Poets In The School program, and taught at the college level since 1989, presently in the Native American Studies programs at Sonoma State University and College of Marin. Awarded Artist in Residence grants from the California Arts Council and the Headlands Center for the Arts, he has also served on various local, state, and national grant and policy review panel, including the California Arts Council and the National Endowment for the Arts. He has received several awards for poetry including the W. A. Gerbode Poetry Award in 1993. He is a founding Board Member of the American Indian Public Charter School in Oakland, CA, and has served as an educational reform consultant for many agencies including the Annenberg Institute for School Reform. He is also a cultural activist, and traditional American Indian singer and an Osage Southern Straight traditional dancer.

Mary Black Bonnet is an enrolled member of the Sicangu Lakota Nation (incorrectly known to the greater world as the Rosebud Sioux Tribe). She was born in Rosebud, South Dakota but taken from her mother at a young age and raised by a non-Native family. She spent the next 22 years trying to get back to her homeland. In her early 20s, she returned, learned her culture and language, and then used it in her work, writing both in Lakota and English. She has been an artist in residence at Colorado College and Leech Lake Tribal College, and a visiting writer at Sinte Gleska University and Ihanktowan College as well as at various schools. She is a feminist author with a strong voice and a long to-do list. "I became a feminist by circumstance," she says. "As long as Native women and children's voices remain unheard, I will use my voice to assist, help them find their strength and voices. The dark ages are over." She has published poetry, and nonfiction essays. Her work can be seen in *Tribal College Journal, Frontiers: a Journal of Women's Studies; Genocide of the Min;, Eating Fire Tasting Blood; Sharing Our Stories: Native women surviving Violence,* and *Birthed From Scorched Hearts.* www.maryblackbonnet.com

Trevino L. Brings Plenty was born on the Cheyenne River Sioux Reservation, Eagle Butte, SD. A Minneconjou Lakota Indian, he lived on the reservation until age three, then with family moved to the San Francisco Bay Area. At age 16, he moved to Portland, OR, where he now resides. He is 55/64 Lakota, the 9/64 is unknown (probably fur trapper). To order his book *Real Indian Junk Jewelry*, got to www.thebackwaterspress.org

Susan Deer Cloud, a mixed lineage Catskill Mountain Indian, is the recipient of an Elizabeth George Foundation Grant, a National Endowment for the Arts Literature Fellowship, two New York State Foundation for the Arts Poetry Fellowships, and a Chenango County Council for the Arts Grant. Her work has been published in numerous literary journals and anthologies; her most recent books are *Fox Mountain Poems, Braiding Starlight, Car Stealer* and *The Last Ceremony*. She likes to eat blueberries in winter and sing to cats. To learn more, you can visit Deer Cloud's website at http://sites.google.com/site/susandeercloud/.

Vine Deloria Jr. (1933–2005) Standing Rock Sioux (SD) steadfastly worked to demythologize how white Americans thought of American Indians. The myths, he often said - whether as romantic symbols of life in harmony with nature or as political bludgeons in fostering guilt - were both shallow. The truth, he said, was a mix, and only in understanding that mix, he argued, could either side ever fully heal. As best-selling author of many acclaimed books including Custer *Died for Your Sins: An Indian Manifesto, God is Red: A Native View of Religion, Evolution and Creationism and Other Modern Myths, Red Earth, White Lies: Native Americans and the Myth of Scientific Fact* and *The World We Used to Live In: Remembering the Powers of the Medicine Men,* Deloria spoke authoritatively on tribal sovereignty and self-determination. As a historian, he promoted Native science amid conflicting Western views. And as an advocate, he worked on countless initiatives, legislative and otherwise, to protect sacred sites, ancestral remains and artifacts and the federal-tribal relationship. Named by *Time* magazine as one of the greatest religious thinkers of the twentieth century, he will forever be remembered as a literary genius, visionary, and groundbreaking Indigenous activist.

Trace A. DeMeyer (Tsalagi-Shawnee-Euro) is an award-winning journalist, former editor of the *Pequot Times* in Connecticut and editor/co-founder of *Ojibwe Akiing*; she freelances for *News from Indian Country* in Wisconsin and maintains several blogs and a Twitter newspaper: *Modern Ndn.* Her book *One Small Sacrifice: A Memoir,* describes little-known history of the Indian Adoption Projects. *Two Worlds: Lost Children of the Indian Adoption Projects*, published in 2012, was co-authored with Patricia Busbee. Her writing, interviews and poetry have been published in newspapers and journals in the USA, Canada and Europe. Trace, a BFA graduate of the University of Wisconsin-Superior, has received numerous news and feature writing awards. www.tracedeyer.com

Phyllis A. Fast, a Koyukon Athabascan born in 1946, has received two literary awards: The 2006 Alaska Conservation Foundation Alaska Native Writer on the Environment Award for "Of Tadpoles and Spruce Pitch" and the 2000 North American Indian Prose Award for *Northern Athabascan Survival: Women, Community and the Future!* published by the University of Nebraska Press in 2002. Fast has a B.A. in English from the University of Alaska, an M.A. in English and Anthropology from the University of Alaska Anchorage, and a PhD in Social Anthropology from Harvard University. After teaching at the University of Alaska Fairbanks for nine years, Fast has been teaching at the University of Alaska Anchorage since 2004.

Jack D. Forbes (1934-2011) of Powhatan-Renapé and Lenápe descent was a writer, scholar and political activist. He is best known for his role in establishing one of the first Native American Studies programs (at UC Davis), and for founding D-Q University, the first Native American college located outside a reservation. He received his Bachelors degree in Philosophy from USC in 1953, going on to a Masters in 1955 and a Ph.D. in History and Anthropology (1959). In the early 1960s, he became one of the first participants and organizers in the Native American movement. He authored many outstanding works including *Columbus and Other Cannibals; The American Discovery of Europe; Red Blood* (Novel); *Only Approved Indians: Stories; Apache, Navaho and Spaniards* and *Africans and Native Americans.*

Odilia Galván Rodríguez, is of Chicano-Lipan Apache ancestry, born in Galveston, Texas and raised on the south side of Chicago. As a social justice activist for many years Ms. Galván Rodríguez worked as a community and labor organizer, for the United Farm Workers of America AFL-CIO and other community based organizations and served on various city/county boards and commissions. She is the author of three books of poetry, of which *Migratory Birds: New and Noted Poems* is her latest. Her creative writing both fiction and poetry, appears in *Reinventing the Enemy›s Language: Contemporary Native American Women›s Writings of North America; New Chicana / Chicano Writing: 1& 2; Here is my kingdom: Hispanic-American literature and art for young people.* She has most recently worked as the English Edition Editor for *Tricontinental Magazine*, in Havana, Cuba under OSPAAAL an NGO, a non-governmental organization, with consultative status to the United Nations. She is also one of the facilitators of Poets Responding to SB1070, a Facebook page dedicated to calling attention to the unjust laws recently passed in Arizona, which target Latinos. Ms. Galván Rodríguez is hard at work on two books of poetry and a collection of short stories and offers Empowering People Through Creative Writing workshops internationally.

Tiokasin Ghosthorse, Lakota, from the Cheyenne River Reservation in South Dakota, has been the host of First Voices Indigenous Radio, (NYC) for the last 21 years. He has a long history with Indigenous activism and advocacy. He is a survivor of the "Reign of Terror" from 1972 to 1976 on the Pine Ridge Lakota Reservation, and the U.S. Bureau of Indian Affairs Boarding and Church Missionary School systems designed to "kill the Indian and save the man." He is also a master musician, having played and a teacher of magical, ancient and modern sounds. He is one of the great exponents of the ancient red cedar Lakota flute, and plays traditional and contemporary music, using both Indigenous and European instruments. He currently sits on Harvard University's "Cultures on the Air" board, which is working to bring Indigenous voices worldwide via radio. http://www.firstvoicesindigenousradio.org/

Bobby González (Taino) is a multicultural lecturer, performance poet and storyteller. Born and raised in the South Bronx, New York City, he grew up in a bicultural environment. Bobby draws on his Native American and Latino roots to offer a unique repertoire of discourses, readings and performances that celebrates his indigenous heritage. Bobby has lectured at many institutions including Yale University, the University of Alaska-Fairbanks and the University of Alabama-Huntsville. As a storyteller he's had the privilege of performing at Carnegie Hall, the Museum of Television & Radio and the Detroit Institute of Arts. He has given poetry readings at the National Museum of the American Indian, the University of North Dakota and the Nuyorican Poets Café. The title of his most recent book is *The Last Puerto Rican Indian: A Collection of Dangerous Poetry*. Bobby González seeks to empower his audiences by encouraging them to embrace their heritage and use this knowledge to create a dynamic future. He is the event coordinator and master of ceremonies for the annual Bronx Native American Festival.

Suzan Shown Harjo is a Cheyenne citizen of the Cheyenne & Arapaho Tribes and is Hodulgee Muscogee of Nuyakv Ground. President of The Morning Star Institute in Washington, DC, she is a poet, writer, curator, lecturer and policy advocate, who has helped Native Peoples protect sacred places and recover more than one million acres of land. She has developed key laws in five decades to promote and protect Native nations, sovereignty, children, arts, cultures and languages, including the *American Indian Religious Freedom Act*, *National Museum of the American Indian Act* and *Native American Graves Protection and Repatriation Act*. Dr. Harjo is the first Native woman to receive an Honorary Doctorate of Humanities from the Institute of American Indian Arts (2011), the first Vine Deloria, Jr., Distinguished Indigenous Scholar (University of Arizona, 2008; and a 2013 Deloria Lecturer), the first person to be awarded back-to-back fellowships by the School of Advanced Research (in Poetry and as a Summer Scholar, 2004) and the first Native woman to be honored as a Montgomery Fellow (Dartmouth College, 1992). Past Executive Director of the National Congress of American Indians, former Legislative Liaison for the Native American Rights Fund and a Founding Trustee of the National Museum of the American Indian, she is Guest Curator and General Editor of NMAI's "Treaties: Great Nations In Their Own Words" (opening and publication, 2014) and an award-winning Columnist for *Indian Country Today Media Network*. She also is the mother of two adult children and the grandmother of two grandsons.

Barbara-Helen Hill is an author/artist from Six Nations of the Grand River in Southern Ontario Canada. She is of mixed ancestry - Cayuga/Mohawk and British Isles. She is the mother of three and the grandmother of four and a great-grandmother of two. Barbara-Helen likes to tell traditional stories in her fabric art pieces as well as her short stories and poems. She is the author of *Shaking the Rattle- Healing the Trauma of Colonization*, and her work has appeared in *Genocide of the Mind: New Native Writings* and *Birthed From Scorched Hearts: Women Respond to War.*

Gabriel Horn, White Deer of Autumn, considers himself *Indigenous*. He is a member of the family of Princess Red Wing, Metacomet, and Nippawanock of the Narragansett Tribe/ Wampanoag Nation. Co-author of *Transcendence* (2012 National Indie Excellence Book Award); *The Book of Ceremonies; Native Heart; Contemplations of a Primal Mind*, and *The Great Change*. Coming soon, *Rainy's Door: an American Indian Novella for the Children of the Earth*. One of the original 1974 teachers at Heart of the Earth AIM Survival School and former Head Teacher at The Red School House, he is a 4 time recipient of Who's Who Among America's Teachers. Professor of literature and creative writing: retired.

Dean Hutchins is of Cherokee ancestry and grew up in City of New York. He attended several colleges but left his studies to become a self-taught systems engineer and internationally known computer consultant. His interest in communications gave him a second career as a writer. His work has been published in *Talking Stick* and *Native Realities*. He has produced television programs of interest to the Native community. Hutchins served on the board of the Native American Education Program of New York City. He is active in New York's traditional Keetoowah community. He is currently living in Arlington, Virginia and writing his first novel.

Basil H. Johnston (13 Jul 1929) O.Ont, LLD, B.A., Anishinaabe writer, storyteller, language teacher and scholar, was born on the Wasauksing First Nation. He is a member of the Chippewas of Nawash Unceded First Nation (formerly known as the Cape Croker Band of Ojibwa). Basil has written 15 books in English and five in Ojibwemowin on his culture to show there is more to North American Indian life than social organization, hunting and fishing, food preparation, clothing, dwellings and transportation; and he has numerous articles published in newspapers, anthologies and periodicals. He is a member of the ethnology department at Royal Ontario Museum, Toronto.

Amy Krout-Horn is the author of *My Father's Blood* (All Things That Matter Press, 2011) and *Transcendence* (All Things That Matter Press, 2009) which won the 2012 National Indie Excellence Award for visionary fiction. Her work has been featured In_*Breath and Shadow, Talking Stick__Native Arts Quarterly, Independent Ink Magazine*, and *Slate and Style*. For more information visit her website: http://www.nativeearthwords.com

Denise Low, second Kansas Poet Laureate, has published over 20 books of poetry and essays, including *Ghost Stories of the New West*, one of the best Native American Books of 2010 by *The* (*Circle*) and a Kansas Notable Book. She is a 2008-2013 board member of Associated Writers and Writing Programs Her poetry blog is http://deniselow.blogspot.com. She directs a Northern Cheyenne ledger for the Plains Indian Ledger Art online project. Her heritages are British Isles, Delaware (various bands), German, and Cherokee.

Natalie Thomas Kindrick born in Rochester NY, of Algonquin/ Iroquois Italian decent, and was raised on the Cattaraugus Indian Reservation by her grandmother. Natalie joined the Army in the late 70's and retired after 24 years of service. She now resides on a farm in Virginia, raising her 6 children.

MariJo Moore (Cherokee/Irish/ Dutch) is an award winning author/poet/editor/anthologist/lecturer/artist/spiritual advisor who has written over twenty books including *A Book of Spiritual Wisdom for all days, The Diamond Doorknob, When the Dead Dream, Red Woman With Backward Eyes and Other Stories*, and *Confessions of a Madwoman*. She is editor of several anthologies including *Genocide of the Mind: New Native Writings, Birthed From Scorched Hearts: Women Respond to War,* and *Eating Fire, Tasting Blood: Breaking the Great Silence of the American Indian Holocaust*. She has a BA in Literature from Tennessee State University/ Lancashire Polytechnic, England. She resides in the mountains of western NC. www.marijomoore.com

Suzanne Zahrt Murphy is a writer and nurse educator. Her articles have appeared in the *Los Angeles Times* (under a different name), *in the San Francisco Chronicle*, and in *Femspec,* a feminist journal. She is of Cherokee, Swedish, Scottish and German heritage. Her blog can be found at shegoetowater. wordpress.com.

Dawn Karima Pettigrew is a Creek/Cherokee novelist, poet, fiction writer, journalist, filmmaker, recording artist and playwright. For seven seasons, she has hosted *Rezervations with Dawn Karima*, a Native American talk show on the Native Voice

One public radio network and its affiliates, Talktainment and NPR. Her first novel, *The Way We Make Sense*, (San Francisco: Aunt Lute, 2002) was a finalist in the North American Native First Book Award Competition (Greenfield Review), First Runner-up in Kent State's Wick Poetry Competition (Student Division), and an Honorable Mention in the National LookingGlass Contest and Kent State Competition. Her second novel, *The Marriage of Saints*, was released as part of the University of Oklahoma's American Indian Studies series (Norman: University of Oklahoma, 2006). She is a shellshaker and a Southern Cloth Traditional Dancer, whose home is the Qualla Boundary Reservation in Cherokee, NC.

Lois Red Elk says, "My daylight hours are split between a life of working and maintaining duties that keep me physically alive, and a life as a D/Lakota human-being thriving on a plane of thinking, praying and walking in my traditional culture. My nighttime is a mixture of writing, dreams and reading. I live in Montana on the Ft. Peck Sioux Reservation."

Doris Seale, Santa/Cree, is co-founder and president of the board of Oyate, a Native organization working to see that Native lives and histories are portrayed honestly. A dedicated educator and fierce activist, Doris was the recipient of the American Library

Association's Equality Award for her life's work in 2001. (She was a children's librarian for forty–five years.) She is the author of *Ghost Dance, Blood Salt,* co-editor of *Through Indian Eyes,* and *A Broken Flute,* which won the American Library Award. Her writings and poetry have appeared in various publications and anthologies. She resides in Vermont.

Keith Secola is an award-winning musician, guitarist and Native flute player, singer, songwriter, and producer. His music is familiar to thousands of fans across North America and Europe. Keith's famous song, "NDN KARS" is considered the contemporary Native American anthem and is the most requested song on Native radio in the US and Canada. Keith Secola is Anishinabe (Ojibwa) originally from the Mesabi Iron Range country of northern Minnesota, now residing in Arizona. He's a member of the Anishinabe Nation of northern Minnesota and southern Ontario, Canada. Secola is a seven-time Native American Music Awards winner receiving numerous Nammy nominations in various categories. In 2011, he was inducted into the Native American Music Awards Hall of Fame.

Stephanie A. Sellers is an American woman of Cherokee, Shawnee, and Sephardic Jewish ancestry. Her poetry and coyote stories have appeared in *American Indian Culture & Research*

Journal Native Literatures: Generations, and forthcoming in *Studies in American Indian Literatures*. She studied with Paula Gunn Allen for her doctoral degree in Native American Studies (2005); her favorite flower is Lilium 'Casa Blanca'; and her preferred Wise Woman herbal ally is Stinging Nettle infusion.

Kim Shuck is a writer, weaver, bead artist and walker on the crests of hills. Her artwork has shown on four continents and her poetry has been published on three. Shuck's first juried publication was in the *En'owken* Journal out of Canada. Her first solo book of poetry, *Smuggling Cherokee*, was published by Greenfield Review Press and won the Diane Decorah award from the Native Writers' Circle of the Americas. She lives in San Francisco with grown children, rescue cats and a disagreeable parrot called Bond. She is of Tsalagi and Carpathian descent.

Ire'ne Lara Silva lives in Austin, TX and identifies as Latina/De-Tribalized Native (Huichol, Comanche, Pueblo according to family stories). Her work has appeared in various journals and anthologies, most recently in *Generations, Mas Tequila Review, Palabra*, and *Yellow Medicine Review*. She is the 2008 recipient of the Gloria Anzaldua Milagro Award, an inaugural CantoMundo Fellow, and the author of two chapbooks: *ani'mal* and *INDíGENA*. Her first collection of poetry, *furia*

(Mouthfeel Press, 2010) received an Honorable Mention for the 2011 International Latino Book Award in Poetry. Currently, she is Co-Coordinator for the Flor De Nopal Literary Festival. http://flordenopalliteraryfestival.wordpress.com/ Poet/writer website: http://www.irenelarasilva.webs.com

Georges Sioui is Huron-Wendat. He was Editor-in-chief of the *Kanatha* magazine, in Wendake (1973-1977) and of the *Tawow* magazine at the Department of Indian and Northern Affairs, in Ottawa (1977-1980). In 1980, he became Assistant-Director General of the Cree Board of Health and Social Services of James Bay, in Chisasibi, Quebec. He obtained an MA in History from Laval University in 1987 and became, in 1991, the first Canadian Amerindian with a Doctoral Degree in History. He has been Dean of Academics at the Saskatchewan Indian Federated College (1993-1997) and President of the Institute of Indigenous Government, in Vancouver (1999-2000). Georges Sioui has initiated and successfully directed with his four brothers the celebrated *Sioui Case* (Supreme Court of Canada, 1990). Georges Sioui has been Head of Research at the Indian Claims Commission (2003) before becoming the Coordinator of the new Program of Aboriginal Studies at the University of Ottawa (2004-2012). Now a Full Professor, he dedicates himself to his teaching, research and writing. He is the author of three landmark books, one of which is *For an Amerindian Autohistory*. Georges Sioui is polyglot, a poet, essayist, songwriter and a world-renowned speaker.

Jim Stevens is a poet of Seneca heritage. He lives in northern Wisconsin

Clifford E. Trafzer, Wyandot, is Professor of History and Director of the California Center for Native Nations at the University of California, Riverside, where he holds the Rupert Costo Chair in American Indian Affairs. Most recently he coedited *The Indian School on Magnolia Avenue: Voices and Images of Sherman Institute* and coauthored *Forgotten Voices: Death Records of the Yakama, 1888-1964*. He is currently researching the medicine ways of Southern California Indians, Yuman tribes of the Colorado River, and Comanche healer Kenneth Coosewoon.

Terra Trevor, Cherokee, Delaware, Seneca, is a widely published essayist, memoirist and nonfiction writer. In addition to writing Terra has worked as a Project Director with American Indian Health Services Red Ribbon Bridge - a program offering spiritual, cultural connection and Indian doctoring for Native Americans living with AIDS, as a coordinator in Seoul, South Korea with Friends of Korea Family Exchange Program, and as a coordinator with Hospice and We Can Pediatric Brain Tumor Network. www.terratrevor.com

John Trudell, musician, poet, activist, is the son of a Santee Sioux father and a Mexican mother, who grew up around the Santee reservation near Omaha. His movies include *Thunderheart, No More Smoke Signals,* and *American's Lost Landscape.* His albums are *AKA Grafitti Man, Bone Days, Johnny Damas and Me, Blue Indians, Live à FIP,* and *Madness & Moremes.*

Lela Northcross Wakely, Pottawatomi, Kickapoo and Irish, is in her late 50's and the youngest of 10 children. She is an L.P.N. and in the Pediatric Home Health field since 1986. A member of Wordcraft Circle of Native Writers & Storytellers, her work as appeared in *Healing Through Words: Poetry...Prose...Prayers... Stories, Turtle Island to Abya Yala- A New Anthology by Native Women, Eating Fire, Tasting Blood: An anthology of the American*

Indian Holocaust, Children of the Dragonfly: Native American Voices on Child Custody and Education, and *Through the Eye of the Deer: An Anthology of Native American Women Writers.* Her hobbies include needlecraft, gardening and bee keeping.

William S. Yellow Robe, Jr. is a member of the Assiniboine Tribe from the Fort Peck Indian reservation located in Northeastern Montana. He is presently a Libra Professor in the English Department at the University of Maine, Orono, Maine, and a Faculty Affiliate in the Creative Writing Department at the University of Montana, Missoula, Montana. He is a company member of the Ensemble Studio Theater of New York, NY, The Penumbra Theater Company, St. Paul, Minnesota, and The American Indian Artists Inc/AMERINDA in New York, N.Y. He is an Advisory Board member for Red Eagle Soaring Theater Company of Seattle, Washington. *Where the Pavement Ends; New Native Drama,* is an anthology of his one- act plays, and *Grandchildren of the Buffalo Soldiers and Other Untold Stories,* is a collection of his full-length plays.

Gratitude

This publication is made possible with funding from the following generous people. Thank all of you so much! *Sgi!*

Charles and Becky Allen, Alice M. Azure,

Carol Willette Bachofner, Byron Ballard, John D. Berry,

Glenda Hamlin Biggs, Deborah A. Bowles, Phyllis Boyer,

Patricia Busbee, Menoukha Case, Susan Deer Cloud,

Olivia Everhardt, Phyllis A. Fast, Bobby González,

Amy Krout-Horn, Gabriel Horn, Dean Hutchins,

Heather M. Jollay, Tommy Kerr, Natalie Thomas Kindrick,

Nickey and Bea Love, Denise Low, Suzanne Z. Murphy,

Marie Nigro, Shelly M. Nixon, Mary Jean Robertson,

Stephanie Sellers, Siobhan Senier, Carrie Sheffield,

Lyndia Stauffer, Wendy Stephens, Jim Stevens, Grace Walsh

rENEGADE pLANETS pUBLISHING is an independently owned business and was chosen as Western North Carolina's Minority Business of the Year in 2007, and Small Press Publisher of the Year 2002 by Wordcraft Circle of Native Writers and Storytellers.

To order books, please go to www.marijomoore.com

20409125R00186

Made in the USA
Charleston, SC
09 July 2013